access to philoso

ISSUES *of* LIFE *and* DEATH

Michael Wilcockson

Hodder Murray

A MEMBER OF THE HODDER HEADLINE GROUP

Some other titles in the series:

Ethical Theory
Mel Thompson   ISBN 0 340 72075 1

Philosophy of Religion
Peter Cole   ISBN 0 340 72491 9

Future titles in the series:

Religion and Science
Mel Thompson   ISBN 0 340 75771 X

Sex and Relationships
Michael Wilcockson   ISBN 0 340 72489 7

Environmental Ethics
Joe Walker   ISBN 0 340 75770 1

Orders: please contact Bookpoint Ltd, 130 milton Park, Abingdon, Oxon OX14 4SB.
Telephone: (44) 01235 827720, Fax: (44) 01235 400454. Lines are open from
9.00–6.00, Monday to Saturday, with a 24 hour message answering service. You can
also order through our website www.hoddereducation.co.uk

British Library Cataloguing in Publication Data
A catalogue record for this title is available from the British Library

ISBN (10) 0 340 724889
ISBN (13) 0978 340 724889

First published 1999

Impression number   10   9   8
Year   2008   2007   2006

Cover photo from Louvre Museum, courtesy of AKG Picture Library

Typeset by Transet Limited, Coventry, England
Printed in Great Britain for Hodder Murray, an imprint of Hodder Education, a
member of the Hodder Headline Group, 338 Euston Road, London, NW1 3BH by
CPI Bath

£7.99

Contents

Preface

To the General Reader

Although *Access* books have been designed mainly to meet the needs of examination students, they also have much to offer the general reader. *Access* authors are committed to writing up-to-date scholarly texts in an easily accessible format. The main body of the text should therefore provide a readable and engaging survey of the subject, in easily digestible sections. Clarity is further enhanced by sub-headings and bulletpoints.

To the Student Reader

Access books are written mainly for students studying for examinations at higher level, particularly GCE Advanced Subsidiary (AS) Level and Advanced (A) Level. A number of features have been included to assist students, such as the word-lists at the beginning of chapters and the material at the end of chapters.

To use this book most effectively, you should be aware of the following features.

- The introductory chapter will set the scene for the material in the rest of the book.
- The Contents gives a breakdown of the sections in each chapter.
- If you turn to the relevant chapters, you will find that they are broken down further into sub-headings and bulletpoints. There are sometimes also Key Issues to focus your attention on important points.
- The Key Words at the beginning of each chapter are for easy reference and to help you become more familiar with the technical language of the subject.
- At the end of each chapter is a Summary of the main points, presented either as lists or diagrams. This is a useful quick revision tool. The list can also form the outline of your own notes on the topic.
- There may be some suggestions for further reading on the topic.
- There is also a range of typical examination questions, with some specific advice on how to answer them. Do tackle the specimen questions, planning your answers to some of them and writing some in full.

General advice on answering essay questions
Structured questions will tell you what to include. The following advice is for those questions which leave it to you to work out.

- The most important thing is to read the question carefully and work out what it really means. Make sure you understand all the words in question (you may need to check some of them in the dictionary or look up technical terms in the Word Lists in the book).

- Gather the relevant information for answering the question. You will probably *not* need everything you know on the topic. Keep to what the question is asking.
- Organise your material by drawing up a plan of paragraphs. Make sure that each paragraph is relevant to the question. Include different views within your answer (most questions require arguments for and against).
- Start with an introduction which explains in your own words what the question is asking and defines any technical words. Work through your answer in your carefully planned paragraphs. Write a brief conclusion in which you sum up your answer to the question (without repeating everything in the essay).

1 Sanctity of Life

1 Sacred lives and valuable lives

> **KEY ISSUE** Why is it wrong to kill people? Is it *always* wrong to kill people? Are some lives more worthwhile than others?

These questions about life, its worth and its value, pose some of the most basic and most difficult problems for any form of morality. The questions are not just deceptively simple but intriguing because our intuitive reactions give equally opposite answers. For instance, we might feel that it is outrageous for a terrorist to kill a shop full of people, but we would have no hesitation in shooting an intruder in our house. On the other hand we might support the right of a couple to conceive a child using artificial means when that money could improve the quality of life of many sick but elderly people.

● Until recently Western morality has explained our special regard for human life through what is termed the **sanctity of life argument** (SOL). The term *sanctity of life* literally means a 'life set aside' because it is created specially and uniquely by God. In other words it argues that human life is **intrinsically** (i.e. in itself) worthwhile, there is no other justification for its value but the fact that it is alive. The Judaeo-Christian basis for the SOL further suggests that humans have a duty to preserve it (a view shared equally by Islamic theology).

● But in recent years two factors have challenged the traditional sanctity of life position. Western society has become more critical of religious claims and advanced medical technology has blurred the boundaries between life and death. As a result many philosophers have proposed a rival viewpoint to the SOL. The proponents of the **valuable life argument** (VLA) or **quality of life argument** (QOL) have argued that SOL does not account adequately for the strongly intuitive feelings about the preservation and value of life, and the equally important sense that humans have of the freedom to dispose of their own lives as they wish. Unlike the SOL, with its premise based on the existence of God, the QOL suggests that the value of life is to do with external or **extrinsic** factors such as the desire to live and the right to die. The chief feature of the QOL is that it removes the *absoluteness* of life and argues that people also have a right to die when they wish.

Take, for example, the following rather bizarre and extreme episode from André Gide's novel *The Vatican Cellars*. Lafcadio is sitting in a train opposite a complete stranger called Fleurissoire. The thought enters his mind that he could – as a complete, unprovoked and free act – kill him. The game, as he calls it, is not to do with the morality of killing, but seeing if he can get away with it.

1   'A crime without a motive,' went on Lafcadio, 'what a puzzle for the police! As to that, however, going along beside this blessed bank, anybody in the next-door compartment might notice the door open and the old blighter's shadow pitch out ... Pooh! if one could foresee
5   all the risks, there'd be no interest in the game!'

A. Gide, *The Vatican Cellars*
(trans. D. Bussy, Penguin edition, 1969) pp. 184–190

In order to make the act even more arbitrary Lafcadio decides that if by the time he has counted to twelve he has not seen a light from a house outside then he will not kill Fleurissoire. He begins to count and at nine he spots a light in a house and without further thought pushes the hapless man out of the carriage to his certain death. So, how are we to judge Lafcadio's action? Did he think that what he had done was morally wrong? Do we imagine that he had any pang of conscience or did he really think that exercising his free will was more important than regard for human life? The incident ends later on that day:

1 When the evening paper came he bought the *Corriere* from the newspaper-seller in the Corso; then he went into a restaurant, but he laid the paper all folded on the table beside him and forced himself to finish his dinner without looking at it – out of a kind of bravado, and as
5 though he thought in this way to put an edge on his desire, then he went out, and once in the Corso again, he stopped in the light of a shop window, unfolded the paper and on the second page saw the following head-line: CRIME, SUICIDE OR … ACCIDENT.

from A. Gide, *The Vatican Cellars*

The story raises a number of important issues concerning the ethics of life and death:

- Is killing human life always wrong? Can we say that killing Fleurissoire was plainly wrong?
- Is it only external factors which make killing wrong (i.e. being caught, fear of reprisals, anger of others, they happen to be your friend or family or member of the community)?
- What constitutes a worthwhile life? For Lafcadio it seems to be a mixture of freedom, bravado and fulfilment of pleasure or desire.
- Are some lives more valuable than others? Lafcadio regards Fleurissoire as an arbitrary and worthless object of his game. Do we do the same in real life? For instance, how can we justify spending thousands of pounds rescuing a child stuck down a well, but allow thousands to die of starvation in a Third World country? Do we think it more or less tragic when a young person dies than an old person?

a) Human beings and human persons

An important distinction to make at this stage is between the biological description of the human being as a member of the species *Homo sapiens* and the human being as a **person**. Ronald **Dworkins** (see his *Life's Dominion*, 1993) usefully employs the two Greek terms for life to clarify this distinction: *zoë* – life as an animal, and *bios* – life as an account of a person's actions and history. Whereas there is no philosophical problem determining when a human may be described as *Homo sapiens*, i.e. as soon the process of biological life begins, his or her *bios* as person presents us with answers that are far less cut and dried.

Furthermore, as Peter **Singer** (see his *Practical Ethics*, 1979) argues, whereas being *Homo sapiens* can only apply to one biological species, being a *person* need not mean one is *Homo sapiens* but could be descriptive of the characteristics of a number of species. When we use the terms 'sanctity of life' or 'valuable life', we mean that these apply to humans as *zoë* but more specifically to human persons. Seeing humans as persons immediately identifies them as moral agents. This is a distinction we know well. During war the enemy are frequently seen as *Homo sapiens* (i.e. as animals) quite separate from the moral human community, and when someone is punished by execution the justification is sometimes argued that their death is no more than putting down a dangerous beast. In both cases people are **dehumanised** so that ordinary human values need not apply in the same way.

But we quite often distinguish *degrees* of person-hood. We sometimes say, 'They are not the person they used to be', or in lamenting the premature death of a baby or child we feel that they have not had time to *develop* their lives, that they have had their personalities 'cut short'. When **Aristotle** (384–322 BCE) discussed what constitutes a person (see his *Ethics*, Book I:1098a27) he concluded with the proverb 'one swallow does not make a summer'. What he meant was that to be a person comprises a series of diverse experiences over a period of time and we cannot point to a moment when someone becomes a person.

The question is: what basic experiences determine a *bios* (life as a person with a history) from mere *zoë* (a life of animal existence as a member of the species *Homo sapiens*)?

b) Basic goods

What basic goods, values or qualities constitute a worthwhile human life as a person? Despite the inherent dangers in drawing up such lists (see Harris, *The Value of Life*, 1985), here are some suggestions from philosophers past and present.

- **John Finnis**: legal philosopher (see his *Natural Law and Natural Rights*, 1980). Finnis lists seven equal basic goods: the desire for a life free from mental and physical pain, knowledge (the desire to find out for its own sake), play, aesthetic experience, sociability (friendship), practical reasonableness (application of intelligence), 'religion' (by which he means that which binds us together in collaboration and community). Finnis makes clear that these are not *moral* goods, but goods which constitute a valuable life.
- **Joseph Fletcher**: moral philosopher in the Christian Protestant tradition. Fletcher is famous for his enormously influential book *Situation Ethics* (1966) in which he lists his 'indicators of humanhood' as: self-awareness, self-control, sense of the future, sense of the past, capacity to relate to others, concern for others, communication, curiosity.
- **John Locke** (1632–1704): British empiricist philosopher. Locke reduces the possible basic goods to one, and that is the ability to think and reflect:

> 1 we must remember what a person stands for; which I think, is a thinking intelligent being, that has reason and reflection, and can consider itself, the same thinking thing, in different times and places; which it does only by that consciousness which is inseparable from
> 5 thinking and seems to me essential to it; it being impossible for any one to perceive without perceiving that he does perceive.

An Essay Concerning Human Understanding (1690), Book II, ch. 27

Locke's position is attractive because of its simplicity and because of the notoriously difficult process of distinguishing the number of basic goods. We can see how many of Fletcher's 'indicators' or Finnis's 'values' might be included in Locke's definition, but the problem, so acute in moral dilemmas of life and death (e.g. abortion and comas), is knowing whether a 'person' is actually functioning as a self-reflecting being.

2 Taking and preserving life: quality of life arguments

Peter Singer represents those who feel that Western ethics can no longer sensibly be based on the sanctity of life suppositions. Singer quotes the following from President Reagan in 1983:

1   Every legislator, every doctor, and every citizen needs to recognize that the real issue is whether to affirm and protect the sanctity of all human life, or to embrace a social ethic where some human lives are valued and others are not. As a nation, we must choose between the sanctity
5   of life ethic and the quality of life ethic.

Rethinking Life and Death (1995), p. 106

Or consider the following attack on the SOL by the philosopher Helga Kuhse:

1   What we have in the qualified sanctity of life principle is a principle that says that it is never permissible intentionally to kill a patient, but that it is sometimes permissible to refrain from preventing her death as long as the latter decision is a means-related one not based on the quality
5   of life in question. But this is where the confusion comes in, because judgements that it is sometimes permissible to withdraw or withhold life-prolonging means are, in fact, based on quality of life criteria that are unarticulated and obtuse.

  When we refrain from preventing the deaths of handicapped infants,
10 comatose patients, and the terminally ill and suffering, by classifying the means necessary for keeping them alive as 'extraordinary', 'not medically indicated', 'disproportionately burdensome', and so on, we are resorting to an equally spurious device in order to preserve our sanctity-of-life ethics unscathed. If we want to go beyond definitional
15 ploys, we must accept responsibility for making life and death decisions on the basis of the quality of life question; we must drop the sanctity of life doctrine and work out a quality of life ethic instead.

The Sanctity of Life Doctrine in Medicine: A Critique (1987), pp. 206–7; 220

However, if the QOL ethic is adopted there is still the difficult task of determining the primary principle which permits or restrains a person taking a life (their own or someone else's). Set out below are five possible essential human qualities which determine whether a life may be taken or preserved. Often one factor implies another, but the question is which provides the most coherent *basis* for moral decision-making.

a) Desires

The desire or will to live is sometimes suggested as a simple way in which to determine whether a person's life is worthwhile. From a **classical utilitarian** point of view (promotion of happiness and avoidance of pain) we might agree that a person who has no desire to live and takes their own life does no wrong since there is no *harm* done to themselves (as they are dead they cannot feel any pain). But there are several reasons why desires are not a satisfactory basis for determining whether life can be taken:

- Many object on *indirect* utilitarian grounds, for instance there may be others who feel pain because of his death.
- Some argue that desires are often unreliable; a temporary state of depression may give the illusion that death is desirable when in fact it is not.
- Direct utilitarianism based on desires gives no satisfactory reasons why a person may not take the life of another if it satisfies his desires. But on indirect utilitarian grounds we might argue that a society where any person's life could be taken by another would be so uncertain that it would cause great anxiety and pain.

b) Preferences

An alternative to the classic utilitarian position based on a pain/pleasure calculus is a version of utilitarianism which promotes the greatest preferences. Singer argues that **preference utilitarianism** gives *direct* reasons why a person's life is respected according to his or her preference to live or die, which is closer to the intuitive response that other human lives should be respected. The advantages with this way of thinking are:

- It permits the taking of another's life if that is his or her wish or preference without having to determine the complexities of rights.
- It protects those whose preference is not to be killed.

c) Autonomy

Many would say that the arguments above could be more coherently expressed without recourse to some kind of utilitarianism. The value of life comes from the ability to determine one's future, that is 'self-rule' or **autonomy**. So, although utilitarianism may value autonomy as the means by which preferences can be made, it is not valuable *in itself* (intrinsically). The value of autonomy as an expression of being a human person has a long history but is particularly significant from the period of the Enlightenment (late seventeenth century) to the present day.

- *Liberalism*: In the nineteenth century J S **Mill** (1806–73) developed what has become the basis of **liberalism** in his famous *On Liberty* (1859). Liberty is the chief means by which a person determines his morality and values. A liberal society avoids 'tyrannising' (Mill's phrase) the minority by the majority, and maximises personal freedoms wherever possible. An expression of liberalism is the ability to take one's own life without interference from the state even if others for whatever reasons regard this to be immoral.
- *Existentialism*: Freedom for Jean-Paul **Sartre** (1905–80) and his **existential** philosophy is the one factor which makes humans different from all other things. Freedom is the imperative to live an *authentic* human life and those who abrogate their freedom cease in a fundamental way to be human and live a false life in 'bad faith' (*mauvaise fois*). Recognising that others are free also unites humans in a common condition; indeed any act of freedom helps to establish freedom for others. However it is far from clear what duties, if any, people have for each other.
- *Kant*: (1724–1804): Whilst existentialism deals uneasily with a 'society' of autonomous beings, Kant's moral philosophy recognises that a desire to act for oneself can only be possible if a person could equally imagine that such an act should be done by all other people. He calls this the **categorical imperative**. So, the presence of a universal **moral law** ensures that individuals are respected for their own sake (as autonomous beings) and protects them from exploitation. So, although autonomy is the chief characteristic of being human it is not licence for any kind of behaviour. It does not, for instance, permit suicide because suicide is the negation of freedom and human value.

The criticism of all liberal systems are that they:

- overvalue personal autonomy at the expense of community;
- fail to take into account the collective morality of society;
- might permit very antisocial behaviour from those who hold extreme views which are in themselves anti-liberal.

d) Rights and contract

Another strand, running alongside advocates of liberalism, is the tradition of social contract. Social contract theories have many different starting points which offer widely divergent accounts of taking and preserving life.

- **Egoism**: Thomas **Hobbes** (1588–1679) in his book *Leviathan* (1651) argued that humans are essentially no different from animals whose primary aim is to survive. Survival is prior to pain/pleasure or concern for others. He argues that survival is the *right* to preserve one's own life at all costs – killing, stealing, adultery are all legitimate means:

  > Every man has a Right to every thing; even to one another's body.

  But the egoist realises that the anarchy which would inevitably follow is not in his best interest. He therefore sacrifices 'his right to all things' in exchange for protection and for peace so as to exercise as much liberty as possible. The role of a state is to ensure that the exchange of rights for contract is maintained. There is, therefore, no intrinsic reason why the taking of life is wrong; for life is protected only insofar as it is in society's best interest to do so. So, David **Hume** (1711–76), who shared some of Hobbes's observations, argued that if a person 'withdraws' from the social contract and takes his own life, then he 'does no harm' to society. He is exercising his right to take his own life.

- Hobbes and, after him, Locke, Rawls (1921–) and many others, have established the *rights* tradition. It is now common to distinguish between *natural rights* (Hobbes's right to life) and *human rights* – rights established through social contract for the welfare of its citizens. Rights enable basic goods to be distributed to each citizen regardless of race or beliefs. An example today of such a contract which serves for many practical purposes is *The Universal Declaration of Human Rights* (1948) drawn up by the United Nations. However, philosophically rights pose problems of equality, justice and distribution. For instance, if it is declared that all people are equal, does a right to home and nationality rank equally with the right to life? We can imagine a situation in a war zone where feeding starving people takes precedence over the right to house those displaced by an invading force, yet both are enshrined as rights in the *Declaration*. And if rights are endowed to people who, as moral agents, can act responsibly, the problem is whether a foetus, an infant, a senile old person or a comatose patient is sufficiently morally aware to exercise those rights in any meaningful way.

e) Life as conscious being

Jonathan **Glover** (*Causing Death and Saving Lives*, 1977) argues against the indirect Utilitarians who claim that the extrinsic side-effects make killing unacceptable (hurt felt by others, loss of hope, etc.) because they fail to credit the intuitive value we place on life itself. Instead he adopts Locke's standpoint and suggests that life is always valuable providing it is a conscious life. Killing is not, therefore, an intrinsic wrong, but wrong because of its 'direct' and detrimental effect on consciousness. A 'life' is not defined simply as a body which is alive in biological terms, but one where consciousness is exercised. Glover takes an *instrumentalist* view of the body; the body is important insofar as it enables conscious experiences to be possible.

> | I have no way of refuting someone who holds that being alive, even though unconscious, is intrinsically valuable. But it is a view that will seem unattractive to those of us who, in our own case, see a life of permanent coma as in no way preferable to death. From a subjective
> 5 point of view, there is nothing to choose between the two.

Causing Death and Saving Lives (1977), p. 45

Killing only takes place when a person is conscious – though Glover gives no grounds as to how one can tell. Length of life is mostly irrelevant to the value of a life, so whilst it is true that a longer life enables a person to fulfil their desires, for others the length of life might be the very factor which makes their life unbearable. It follows, therefore, that a conscious life is a valuable life and should be preserved.

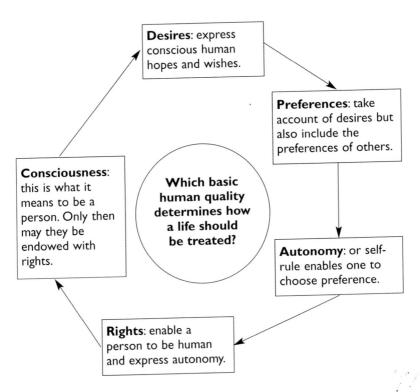

Desires: express conscious human hopes and wishes.

Preferences: take account of desires but also include the preferences of others.

Consciousness: this is what it means to be a person. Only then may they be endowed with rights.

Which basic human quality determines how a life should be treated?

Autonomy: or self-rule enables one to choose preference.

Rights: enable a person to be human and express autonomy.

So, is the QOL or valuable life argument really as persuasive as Peter Singer and Helga Kuhse suggest? John Harris concludes:

1 Even if we felt confident that we could find a very general account of
what makes life valuable for human beings, perhaps by singling out the
most important or most frequently occurring features from the lists of
what they value of a large cross-section of people, we would have no
5 reason to suppose we had arrived at a satisfactory account. For one
thing, people's reasons for valuing life might well change over time; but
more importantly, there would be no reason to suppose that our list
bore any relation at all to the account that might be given of the value
of life by non-human people, people in other worlds.

J. Harris, The Value of Life (1985), pp. 15–16

The alternative is to suggest that life is intrinsically worthwhile, and
that is what has traditionally been considered as the SOL argument.

3 Taking and preserving life: sanctity of life arguments

Sanctity of life arguments in the West are primarily, though not
exclusively, the province of Christian traditions. Within Christian
traditions there are many versions of the SOL argument because
although the basic proposition is that life is sacred and given to
humans by God, modern medical advances have made it increasingly
difficult to determine whether a person has reached a stage where
'life', in any proper sense of the notion, is still a life. Some suggest
that this is really just another version of the QOL argument – there is
fierce discussion whether this is so, and whether it matters. Those
who hold to a **strong SOL** view fiercely defend the SOL against all
humanistic or utilitarian effects which dilute or attempt to dilute or
modify it. A number of terms are used to define their position. One
popular phrase is the **pro-life** group (this is not a term for an
organisation, although you will frequently hear, of a group which is
said to be 'pro-life', or the press use the phrase 'pro-life lobby').
Another more philosophical term is **vitalism**. In its strong form
vitalism argues that a 'life is a life' and that there are no *ordinary or
extraordinary* means which justify the termination of a human life
(even from conception).

a) Biblical basis for the SOL

The SOL appeals to a number of biblical ideas. Specific texts and
passages are clearly more significant when the Bible norm is applied
to specific moral situations. The following selection of texts and ideas
illustrate the main characteristics of the Christian SOL position:

● Image of God

> So God created man in his own image, in the image of God he created man.
>
> Genesis 1:27

> Be fruitful and multiply, and fill the earth and subdue it; and have dominion over every living thing that moves upon the earth.
>
> Genesis 1:28

> And the Word became flesh and dwelt amongst us, full of grace and truth.
>
> John 1:14

Christian anthropology regards each and every human as created in the image and likeness of God. To be created in God's image implies that humans are set apart and different from all other creatures and (Genesis 1:28) possess a 'spark' of divinity within them which enables them to act, create and cultivate the earth as God's stewards. All that God creates is necessarily good. The incarnation of the Word of God as man in the person of Jesus reaffirms the sanctity and holiness of human life in its relationship with God (John 1:14).

● Destiny

> Naked I came from my mother's womb, and naked shall I return; the Lord gave and the Lord has taken away; blessed be the name of the Lord.
>
> Job 1:21

> 1   Therefore I tell you, do not be anxious about your life, what you shall eat or what you shall drink, nor about your body, what you shall put on. Is not life more than food, and the body more than clothing? Look at the birds of the air; they neither sow nor reap nor gather into barns, and yet
> 5   your heavenly Father feeds them. Are you not of more value than they are?
>
> Matthew 6:25–6

If God is the author of life then it follows that He is the one who determines when it should end. Thus in all ordinary circumstances it is not up to the individual whether he or she might add or subtract from his or her life, or anyone else's for that matter. The notion that God is a providential God who has an active role in the universe for good is an important theological presupposition.

● Choose Life

> You shall not kill.
>
> Exodus 20:13

> I call heaven and earth to witness against you this day, that I have set before you life and death, blessing and curse; therefore, choose life.
>
> Deuteronomy 30:19

Running throughout the Bible is the command not to take life. Taking a life is broader than simply killing and the prohibition in the Ten Commandments not to kill is to be seen in the wider setting of respect for parents, for property of others, and relationships with wife, husband and neighbour. The injunction in Deuteronomy 30:19 to 'choose life' is the believer's response to honour God and His creation. The biblical writers see this in terms of a *covenant* relationship between God and His people, that is, a special two-way relationship in which God loves and nurtures people in exchange for their obedience.

● **Love**

> For God so loved the world that he gave his only Son, that whoever believes in him should not perish but have eternal life.
>
> John 3:16

> If anyone has the world's goods and sees his brother in need, yet closes his heart against him, how does God's love abide in him? Little children, let us not love in word or speech but in deed and truth.
>
> I John 3:17–18

> Love bears all things, believes all things, hopes all things, endures all things.
>
> I Corinthians 13:6

Love requires the Christian to respect and protect all humans regardless of status, gender and age (famously illustrated in Jesus' parable of the Good Samaritan in Luke 10:29–37). The Greek term often used by the New Testament is '*agape*' and in its Christian usage suggests that love is active and requires a person to sacrifice his or her own greatest happiness for others (I John 3:17–18 and look also at St Paul's description of love in I Corinthians 13). The model for love is the life, death and resurrection of Christ (John 3:16) in His sacrifice for the good of all.

Jerome **Wernow** (in Kilner *Bioethics and the future of medicine* 1995) summarises four reasons why QOL is rejected in favour of the SOL amongst most conservative Christian medical practitioners:

● The QOL permits too much group pressure and power.
● The QOL inevitably leads to a slippery slope or wedge argument whereby killing humans initially for good reasons inevitably results in less good reasons being adopted in other cases.
● QOL reduces a person's autonomy. Doctors can refuse treatment because *they* think that a patient's life is no longer worthwhile, or the patient senses that they have become burdensome or worthless.
● QOL fails to treat humans with equal dignity.

b) Weak sanctity of life arguments

The main problems of SOL lie not so much in the principles but in the applications to situations which become more and more complicated as medical science blurs the boundaries between life and death. Some supporters of SOL appeal to **extraordinary means** as a justification for killing when life is no longer *quantifiably* worthwhile:

- physical conditions are irreversible;
- diseases are acutely terminal;
- death is imminent.

In this case the absolute prohibition of killing is put in the context of the Christian principle of love, charity and compassion, and acknowledges that killing is neither an intrinsic wrong nor the preservation of life an intrinsic good. Those who criticise the **weak SOL** feel that it has smuggled in the principles of the QOL or valuable life arguments but refused to call them 'valuable', preferring instead 'quantifiable' criteria. Finally, there are those who take the view that the QOL and SOL may be combined where the conclusions are not dissimilar to those adopted by Glover. Jerome Wernow, for instance, argues (in what he calls 'Transcendental SOL') that being alive, in a Christian sense, means living life in body and soul as a 'living sacrifice' (see Romans 12:1). Being 'alive' is not enough unless that person can express himself spiritually and physically (compare to Glover's view above, page 9). Wernow concludes that 'the voice of a transcendent sanctity of life permits both biological and spiritual vitality to be heard in harmony' (in Kilmer, p. 106). A person who is unable to express themselves fully to God might justifiably say that his life has ceased to be valuable.

Answering structured and essay questions

Summary

Exam questions might be very general about the taking of life and the circumstances in which this might occur. Your answer will almost certainly need to refer to ideas and examples from subsequent chapters in this book. This chapter may also be used to answer questions about personal choice, what constitutes a worthwhile life and the traditional meaning of the term *sanctity of life*.

1 *Debate*: The debate between the sanctity of life (SOL) arguments and quality of life (QOL) arguments. Peter Singer argues that SOL is no longer workable and has even been abandoned by religious people. Is killing always wrong?

Human persons: what are the biological and philosophical distinctions between a human being and being a human person (you might want to look ahead to the chapters on abortion and euthanasia)? Views of Dworkins, Singer, Aristotle.

Basic goods: what are the basic human experiences which make a life worthwhile? Views of Finnis, Fletcher, Locke.

2 *Taking life, quality of life arguments:* when may a life be taken, what is the determining factor? Helga Kuhse's QOL argument. In each case consider the difference between direct killing and indirect killing.

   a) desires – views of classical utilitarianism (happiness v. pain);
   b) preferences – views of preference utilitarianism;
   c) autonomy – Mill, Sartre, Kant;
   d) rights – Hobbes and social contract;
   e) consciousness – Locke and Glover.

Weaknesses of the QOL argument: Harris's views.

3 *Sanctity of life arguments:* pro-life or vitalism rejection of ordinary and extraordinary means. This is essentially a religious argument having its roots in the Judaeo-Christian tradition in the West.

   a) Biblical basis of the SOL: image of God, destiny, choosing life, love (*agape*);
   b) SOL v. QOL: four reasons including wedge argument;
   c) Weak SOL: this version of SOL takes into account difficult situations. Being alive from a Christian perspective also means living a worthwhile or fruitful life.

Questions

1a Explain what is meant by the term 'the sanctity of life'.
1b To what extent has modern life made the sanctity of life argument impossible to maintain?
2a Explain what is meant by the terms 'quality of life' or 'valuable life'.
2b Assess the strengths and weaknesses of quality of life arguments in life and death situations.
3 'Most acts of killing people would be wrong in the absence of harmful side-effects' (Glover). Assess Glover's view that killing is usually 'directly wrong'. Is he right to reject the 'sanctity of life' argument?
4 What are the practical implications of Kant's categorical imperative for the ethics of life and death?
5 Is it possible to hold a vitalist or strong sanctity of life argument without contradictions?
6 'As a nation, we must choose between the sanctity of life ethic and the quality of life ethic' (Ronald Reagan). Is the issue as simple as this?

Essay skills

In general for essays of this type your opening paragraphs might explain why there is tension between SOL and QOL arguments. You might wish to suggest that people in the West have become less religious or that technology has made decisions about the preservation of life increasingly complicated. All essays of this general kind are helped by having *examples*. Examples can be from novels, newspapers or one you have made up. Make sure your example is *brief* and *relevant*. Make sure you use technical expressions, you do not need to explain these, unless the explanation helps to further the argument. You may find it easier to do questions from this chapter once you have read other chapters in this book which will provide you with examples.

'Most acts of killing people would be wrong in the absence of harmful side-effects' (Glover). Assess Glover's view that killing is usually 'directly wrong'. Is he right to reject the 'sanctity of life' argument?

Your opening paragraph may want to pose the problem in this way. If life is not sacred or God-given why is killing wrong? This is an essay about a non-religious quality of life argument. Glover's quotation suggests that there has to be a basic reason why we should not kill each other. You can mention here the arguments you want to consider, e.g. preference utilitarianism, rights and autonomy.

In the following paragraphs you should argue and evaluate each of these. You might then wish to consider what he means by side-effects. You could discuss Lafcadio from Gide's novel (or another fictional or real example). Is the only concern which stops us killing being found out and punished or fear of reprisal/revenge? What other side-effects could there be? In the cases of suicide or murder it might be a sense of loss or anger. You could go on to consider Glover's own view that because we value consciousness we respect it in others and this gives us a direct reason why conscious life should not be removed.

Finally, why should the sanctity of life argument be rejected? You could argue that his conclusion is very close to the image of God propositions in the SOL. Does the SOL require a *further* belief in God which makes it incoherent to a non-believer? Does the QOL simply raise further problems about what constitutes a worthwhile life?

2 Suicide and Autonomy

1 Moral reactions to suicide

> **KEY ISSUE** When using the term 'suicide' moral judgements can vary depending on what kind of suicide is being discussed.

In many people's minds there is no particular moral issue concerning suicide. In modern terms a person has the right freely to dispose of his or her life as he or she wishes. This in itself is significant and illustrates one of the chief characteristics of a liberal society. However, on closer inspection, the debate is not nearly as clear-cut as it first seems. Many of those who have experience of a friend or family member who has committed or attempted suicide do not regard it as an expression of a right but as a selfish and degrading act.

Christian teaching, whilst sympathetic to the state of mind a person might be in, regards suicide as an act of defiance against the will of God; the atheist existentialist sees suicide as an act which denies authentic existence and is an act of bad faith. So, what may be said in general and held to be acceptable in public is not always borne out in the particular.

The term 'suicide' was coined in the seventeenth century from two Latin words '*sui*' – self and '*cidium*' – murder. Other terms include 'self-murder', 'self-destruction' and 'self-slaughter'. But when using the term 'suicide' moral judgements can vary depending on what kind of suicide is being discussed. For the purposes of this topic we shall limit suicide to mean the taking of one's own life without the involvement of a third party. The question of **assisted suicide** has its own legal and moral problems which will be considered under **euthanasia** in chapter 4.

a) Suicide and society

The history of social attitudes to suicide also gives us an insight into shifting attitudes to the place of the Church, the law and class structures. For instance, in the sixteenth century a suicide was buried at the crossroads with a stake through the heart, and in many European countries suicide meant automatic loss of property. In France, for instance, during the late seventeenth century a nobleman who had committed suicide was reduced to the rank of a commoner, his castles demolished and his estate passed to the crown. But during the period of the Enlightenment, with its emphasis on *reason*, philosophers considered whether suicide was perhaps an act against the state rather than nature or God. By the time of the French Revolution (1789), their conclusions must have been accepted for the suicide laws had by this time been dropped.

But the social taboo against suicide held fast in many societies and, for example, it was not until 1961 that the last anti-suicide laws were removed in the UK (following the strong recommendation of the Church of England's Christie Committee in 1960). The law had effectively, and for some time, been circumvented by lawyers using the phrase that a suicide had died whilst 'the balance of his mind was unsound'. The phrase indicates another influence in moral reasoning. For almost a century **psychology** had helped to replace taboo in moral reasoning and was gaining increasing importance in the public perception of suicide. In most cases the phrase 'unsound mind' was the means to safeguard the suicide victim from the punishment which would logically follow a murder. The shift in law recognised that a major moral taboo had finally come to an end after

1500 years of discrimination. Even so, as late as 1969 a boy was birched on the Isle of Man for attempted suicide.

An example from nineteenth-century England illustrates how increasingly people found punishment absurd and ridiculous. In 1860 Nicholas Ogarev wrote to his mistress, Mary Sutherland, commenting on the following news from the London newspapers. The papers had merely commented on the slightly bizarre occurrence, not the suicide itself. But for Ogarev the event said a great deal about *society*:

> 1 A man was hanged who had cut his throat, but who had been brought back to life. They hanged him for suicide. The doctor had warned them that it was impossible to hang him as the throat would burst open and he would breathe through the aperture. They did not listen to his advice
> 5 and hanged their man. The wound in the neck immediately opened and the man came back to life again though he was hanged. It took time to convoke the aldermen to decide the question of what was to be done. At length aldermen assembled and bound up the neck below the wound *until he died*. Oh my Mary, what a crazy society and what a
> 10 stupid civilisation.

A. Alvarez (1974), *The Savage God*, p. 63

2 Philosophical considerations

The philosophical views of suicide were developed first amongst the Greeks and then applied in cruder form by the Romans. In general Greek society rejected suicide because it was regarded as a treacherous act against the state and equated with the same moral outrage as killing a member of the family. But other forms of suicide were commended as being acts of virtue. Homer included it as an act of heroism and Aegeus who threw himself into the sea gave his name to that sea.

a) Plato (*c.* 428–*c.* 348 BCE)

Plato distinguishes between **egoistic** and **altruistic** suicide. In the former case Plato continued the line of thinking which he inherited from the Pythagorians and incorporated it into his notion of the soul. The soul has its origins with the gods and at birth dwells in the body until death at which stage it is deemed pure enough to enter into oblivion or, if insufficiently worthy, is reborn into a new body. Suicide, therefore, is regarded as an act of defiance against the gods and the moral order. The analogy that is often repeated is that suicide is like the soldier who abandons his duty and deserts the battlefield.

We must not put an end to ourselves until God sends us some compulsion like the one we are facing now.

Phaedo 61C–62D

But Plato's view is greatly modified by the death of Socrates, his philosophy master and teacher. Socrates had been condemned to death by the state for corrupting the morals of young Athenians. He was allowed by way of mitigation to take his own life. Socrates' death therefore was not an act of defiance against the gods but on the contrary the death of a man who died *because* of his moral integrity and his belief in the truth. So, without actually calling it **altruistic suicide**, Plato permitted self-death in cases where the individual had displayed a selfless act of moral virtue and not taken an easy escape from a difficult situation.

b) Aristotle (384–322 BCE)

Aristotle considered suicide in the context of the city or '*polis*'. The individual exists not to perfect his soul for after-life, as in Plato's philosophy, but to promote the common good. The primary end of man is to be happy in communion with others. Suicide therefore breaks two important aspects of civilised life. Firstly, it pollutes the state not only as an act against the gods but also as a rejection of the laws of that city. Secondly, the city loses an economically valuable member of that society. The Aristotelian model of society may sound unduly cold and contractual, but it suggests an important principle in that the individual does not act alone in his moral decision-making but must constantly consider the obligations he has to society and society to him.

c) The Stoics (third century BCE)

The Stoics developed Plato's altruistic principle of the noble or heroic death. Unlike Plato they did not share a notion of the after-life, so that self-killing became the crowning act of reason over weaker emotions. This may sound like a licence to kill, but in practice the Stoic had to prove that his case was reasonable to the Senate before he could commit suicide.

d) Christianity

Christian theology and philosophy eventually developed their own teaching on suicide based to a large extent on the classical philosophers. This was due in part to a lack of explicit teaching on such matters in the Bible and because, in the early years of Christian expansion, Greek philosophy had almost as much influence as the

Bible. After an initial period when the church in some quarters positively encouraged altruistic suicide or martyrdom, St **Augustine** (354–430 AD) effectively broke the trend and set a standard which was to become the guiding principle for the Church until this century. He restated Plato, only this time life is a gift from the Christian God and to die at one's own hands is to usurp the authority of God and of the Church. The other mainstay of Western Christian philosophy, **Aquinas** (1225–74) restated the Augustinian position but in Aristotelian terms as an act against justice and charity. (See below page 25 for theological considerations.)

e) The Enlightenment (eighteenth century)

During the period of the Enlightenment the issue of suicide again became a preoccupation of philosophers anxious to reassert the place of reason as the classical philosophers had done. They were shocked by the excess of the law and the barbaric rites attached to the punishment of suicides. **Voltaire** (1694–1778) in France and David **Hume** (1711–76) in Britain both wrote and commented on suicide.

i) David Hume

Hume's essay is of particular significance because, as with so much of his writings, he expresses a view well before his time. As a philosopher he represents what we would now call a **liberal** view of society, which others such as Mill and Bentham were to develop further in the nineteenth century. The principle of liberalism is to permit the individual as much freedom as possible but with consideration for the needs of others, as J S Mill put it:

> Over himself, over his own body and mind the individual is sovereign.
>
> J S Mill *On Liberty* (edited M Warnock, p. 135).

Hume's moral philosophy (a form of **ethical egoism**) is likewise motivated in the most general terms by a sense of **general benevolence** (or 'sympathy') and a tolerance of traditions and customs providing these do not impinge unduly on the freedom of the individual. Hume's precise logic and powerful prose cut away the arguments to the basics so that wherever he saw excess moral restriction he sought to reduce its influence. The following characterise his moral philosophy:

● First, Hume dismissed the first principle of many moral philosophers that morality is based on Natural Law and observation. Nature gives a number of conflicting imperatives which humans mistakenly take to indicate what is the right way of behaving. Besides often giving contradictory commands there is also a philosophical error. Those who do so commit a **category mistake**, that is, of confusing *first order* observations of fact (nature) with *second order* judgements of value (morals). Morals cannot be derived from nature.

● Secondly, religion is very often of little help. God's will cannot be known by reason. If God acts in the world then everything that happens is God's will, in which case morally we are no better off (because nature is contradictory). Alternatively, if God does not act in the world, then His existence is of little concern to us.

● Thirdly, morality is mostly a question of *social contract*. Hume noted that most social customs evolved from the complex relations surrounding ownership of property. Morality is therefore essentially a process of negotiation. The laws of the land stem from an attempt to maintain and maximise these arrangements (see page 8).

Hume's philosophy has been called *sceptical*. This does not mean he is cynical or negative. The sketch above suggests that he was not in any proper sense a Christian, although his view of human nature suggests that given the right conditions, humans often seek to promote each other's good. His essay 'On Suicide' (1784), which was published after his death, is an excellent example of Hume's philosophical fluency, his wit and radicalism. His conclusion is most significant and modern-sounding:

> A man who retires from life, does no harm to society: He only ceases to do good. Why may I not cut short these miseries at once by an action which is no more prejudicial to society?

Here we have an antithesis to Aristotle's social obligation of the individual to the state, a denial of Plato's rejection of egoist suicide and a repudiation of the Christian teaching of suicide as **mortal sin**. Hume was quite conscious that his essay was a response to all these traditions and an echo of another equally fluent advocate of suicide, Seneca. The significance of suicide for Hume and Seneca is that more than anything else it is the one act where the individual can decisively exercise his **autonomy**. The following are fuller extracts from his essay. Consider what Hume means by the underlined phrases and whether you agree with them.

1 If Suicide be criminal, it must be a transgression of our duty either to God, our neighbour, or ourselves – To prove that suicide is no transgression to our duty to God the following considerations may perhaps suffice. In order to govern the material world, the almighty
5 Creator has established general and immutable laws by which all bodies, from the greatest planet to the smallest particle of matter, are maintained in their proper sphere and function. To govern the animal world, he has endowed all living creatures with bodily and mental powers; with senses, passions, appetites, memory and judgement, by
10 which they are impelled or regulated in that course of life to which they are destined. These two distinct principles of the material and animal world, continually encroach upon each other, and mutually retard or forward each other's operations ... Man is stopped by rivers in his passage over the surface of the earth; and rivers, when properly

15 directed, lend their force to the motion of machines, which serve to the use of man ... All events in one sense may be pronounced the action of the Almighty; they all proceed from those powers with which he has endowed his creatures ... The fall of a tower, or the infusion of a poison, will destroy a man equally with the meanest creature ... Since
20 therefore the lives of men are for ever dependent on the general laws of matter and motion, is a man's disposing of his life criminal, because in every case it is criminal to encroach upon these laws or disturb their operation? ... <u>Has not every one of consequence, the free disposal of his own life?</u> And may he not lawfully employ that power with which
25 nature has endowed him? In order to destroy the evidence of this conclusion, we must show reason, why this particular case is excepted; is it because human life is of so great importance, that 'tis a presumption for human prudence to dispose of it? <u>But the life of a man is of no greater importance to the universe than that of an oyster</u> ...
30 If I turn aside a stone which is falling upon my head I disturb the course of nature, and I invade the peculiar province of the Almighty by lengthening out my life ... <u>When I fall upon my sword, therefore, I receive my death equally from the hands of the Deity as if it had proceeded from a lion, a precipice, or a fever</u> ... For my part I find that
35 I owe my birth to a long chain of causes, of which many depended upon the voluntary actions of men. Let us now examine, according to the method proposed, whether Suicide be of this kind of actions, and be a breach of our duty to our neighbour and to society.

    <u>A man who retires from life, does no harm to society: He only</u>
40 <u>ceases to do good</u>; which if it is an injury, is of the lowest kind – All our obligations to do good to society seem to imply something reciprocal. I receive the benefits from society and therefore ought to promote its interests, but when I withdraw myself altogether from society, can I be bound any longer? ... Why may I not cut short these
45 miseries at once by an action which is no more prejudicial to society? That suicide may often be consistent with interest and with our duty to ourselves, no one can question, who allows that age, sickness, or misfortune may render life a burden, and make it worse even than annihilation. <u>I believe that no man ever threw away life,</u>
50 <u>while it was worth keeping</u>. For such is our natural horror of death that small motives will never be able to reconcile us to it ... If suicide be a supposed crime, 'tis only cowardice can impel us to it.

                             Hume, 'On Suicide' (1784)

ii) Immanuel Kant

Contrary to the liberalism of Hume, Kant's (1724–1804) secular version of the sanctity of life argued that suicide was wrong because it would be contrary to the universal duty (or moral law) to preserve life. For the argument to work Kant assumes *a priori* that a stable society in which members can be happy self-evidently depends on the duty to preserve life. A duty to kill oneself would therefore undermine the stability of society on which the duty to life depends. The key to Kant's argument is that rationally we know a law seeks to be consistent and universal (his **categorical imperative**). A selfish 'law' is neither consistent nor universal and so cannot be a law. Kant couches that argument as a logical impossibility: from self-love I wish to abolish self. If I love myself it is not possible to destroy the object of my love. Alternatively, suicide undermines Kant's **practical imperative** never to treat people as a means to an end. If suicide treats oneself as a means of escape, it would clearly not be respecting self. Despite the problems inherent in the categorical imperative, there is something psychologically persuasive in Kant's observation that suicide *does* undermine the stability of society (the effect on family and friends and so on). On the other hand, it is possible to see some forms of suicide as great acts of dignity without disrespect for self.

1   A man reduced to despair by a series of misfortunes feels sick of life but is still so far in possession of his reason that he can ask himself whether taking his own life would not be contrary to his duty to himself. Now he asks whether the maxim of his action could become a
5   universal law of nature. But the maxim is this:

> from self-love I make as my principle to shorten my life when its continued duration threatens more evil than it promises satisfaction.

There only remains the question as to whether this principle of self-love can become a universal law of nature. One sees at once a
10 contradiction in a system of nature whose law would destroy life by means of the very same feeling that acts so as to stimulate the furtherance of life, and hence there could be no existence as a system of nature. Therefore, such a maxim cannot possibly hold as a universal law of nature and is, consequently, wholly opposed to the supreme
15 principle of all duty.

Kant, Grounding for the Metaphysics of Morals (1785), p. 30

f) Existentialism

i) Jean-Paul Sartre

Freedom is the essential human experience according to the mid-twentieth-century existential philosophers and writers. We are born free, as Jean-Paul Sartre (1905–80) states, and it is only by exercising our will that we become anything. There are no *a priori* morals that we have to conform to, no God to whom we owe any duties, even parents and society have no authority over who we are or should be. Sartre's novels constantly ridicule the morality of the bourgeoisie (the middle classes) and their hypocritical assent to traditional morality. We exist *pour soi* – for ourselves, there is no other being (as far as we know) who exists in this way. Sartre argues that only existentialism maintains the real 'dignity of man'. All other things exist *en soi*, fixed by what they are and unable to change their nature. Humans have no nature except the ability to choose. Ironically, having dismissed all moral imperatives, Sartre is left with one: we must choose in order to exist.

If there are no moral and social *a priori* judgements, can suicide be an option for the existentialist? As existentialism is not a doctrine nor a prescription, the reasons are varied. At the end of *Existentialism and Humanism* (1948) Sartre concludes that actions can only be judged according to freedom (p. 53):

> There are no means of judging. The content is always concrete, and therefore unpredictable; it has always to be invented. The one thing that counts, is to know whether the invention is made in the name of freedom.

He gives his example from George Eliot's *The Mill on the Floss*, where Maggie Tulliver, thwarted in her love, 'instead of heedlessly seeking her own happiness, chooses in the name of human solidarity to sacrifice herself and to give up the man she loves'. At the end of the novel Maggie dies in the act of saving others whilst taking enormous risks on the flooded river. Sartre does not condemn altruistic suicide because death was not the primary aim; it was an expression of freedom.

ii) Albert Camus

But what of **egoistic suicide**? Albert Camus (1913–60) sets out to consider whether killing oneself could be considered the greatest expression of human freedom and the fundamental question for all philosophers. His essay, *The Myth of Sisyphus* (1946), was written shortly after the end of the Second World War when many felt that the war had achieved freedom but at a huge cost in terms of human life. So many had died, so was life worth living? Camus retells the classical story of Sisyphus who is condemned to an eternity of hauling his stone in the underworld to the top of the mountain, where for a brief moment it hovers before rolling back to the bottom. The story considers that if life is essentially meaningless or **absurd** then maybe the only option is suicide. But, Camus argues, it is in grappling with absurdity (the stone) that Sisyphus learns to enjoy and appreciate his predicament. It is by mastering the absurd that a person comes to appreciate true happiness by grasping **despair** and turning it into his *own* goal or fate. Suicide denies the creative freedom to master absurdity and be happy. Despair, rather than faith, reduces man to an unthinking thing, which he is not.

> There is no sun without shadow, and it is essential to know the night. The absurd man says yes and his effort will henceforth be unceasing. For the rest, he knows himself to be the master of his days.

> A. Camus, *Myth of Sisyphus*, p. 110

Camus' justification for rejecting suicide is a poetic humanism. His argument is mystical and depends on the poet's licence to personify absurdity as something almost objective and real. The absurd world of Camus and Sartre is without God but their acceptance of life and rejection of suicide in the end comes very close to traditional Christian theological thinking.

3 Theological considerations

The Christian theological argument begins with the kind of assertions which are summarised as the sanctity of life argument (SOL). As we have noted (see pp 10–12) the SOL reinforces the importance of life as something which is God-given in the same way that creation itself depends for its existence on the will of God. The Judaeo-Christian tradition of the Old and New Testaments constantly reasserts that human life is the means by which humans are able to exercise God's will over creation (Genesis 1:26ff and 9:1–3) and to live in love with their neighbour. The Bible does not explicitly prohibit suicide although it is clear that those who take their lives through their own selfish acts (egoistic suicide) are frowned on, whilst the very few who are called on to give up their lives as an act of altruistic suicide (i.e. as martyrs) are considered to have performed a supreme act of love and devotion to God.

- Death is the punishment for sin (Revelation 20:14): to opt for death is thus to embrace sin rather than overcome it. Death is the enemy of life (Psalm 18:4), the realm of Satan (Hebrews 2:14), and it is only through the redemption of God in the resurrection of Christ that death loses its tragic quality (1 Corinthians 15:54, Philippians 3:10, 2 Corinthians 5:4). On one level death is not a release from suffering, it is the assurance of resurrection which transforms death just as a seed is buried and is transformed into a plant says St Paul, so the death and resurrection of Christ turns finite life into a life of hope.
- Altruistic death, a death out of love (or to use the Greek term often used by the New Testament writers, *agape*) for others is, on the other hand, commended as the supreme act of faith for others. 'Greater love has no man than this, that he lay down his life for his friends' (John 15:13). The writer of Hebrews (11:32–38) cites the death of Samson in the Old Testament (Judges 16:23ff) as a great act of faith. Samson had used his great strength to pull down the building he was chained to, killing himself and the Philistines, his enemies. His action was in response to God's will over Dagon, the pagan god of the Philistines.
- Though not commented on explicitly, egoistic suicide is often seen as the result of God's **judgement**. King Saul dies by falling on his own sword (1 Samuel 31:4) having disobeyed God's laws (1 Samuel 13:8f) and Jeremiah 8:3 considers suicide to be the preferable option for those who have failed to keep to God's laws.

a) St Augustine (354–430 CE)

The most influential and significant argument against suicide was developed by St Augustine. To make sense of Augustine's strong rejection of martyrdom, various factors need to be taken into consideration. Firstly, Tertullian and then the Donatists (a fourth-century Christian heretical movement), amongst others, had actively encouraged martyrdom as a sign of faith and in imitation of Christ's sacrificial death. Secondly, Roman culture had made suicide socially acceptable and Augustine wanted to distance the Church from *pagan* practice and give Christianity its own special moral stance. Because the Bible has no explicit teaching on suicide, Augustine's argument employs Plato's defence from the *Phaedo* which he used to reinterpret biblical texts. His argument is set out in various places, the following can be found in *The City of God* (412–27 CE):

- Killing is condemned under the sixth commandment (Exodus 20:13):'You shall not kill'.
- Self-killing is murder and doubly wrong because, firstly, only executions may be carried out under the authority of the state/Church and suicide is a private act, and secondly, a guilty man cannot condemn a guilty man or, if he is innocent, it is against Natural Law to condemn the innocent to death.
- An untimely death allows no time for repentance for the act of killing. Judas's suicide (Matthew 27:3–5) confirms to us that Judas was indeed a despicable person (having betrayed Christ).
- Self-killing indicates a rejection of God's providence and love.
- Suicide is not a sign of bravery (as the Stoics claim) or strength of spirit but weakness. This life is preparation for the next (as Plato argues in the *Phaedo*) and real strength of character comes when hardships have been endured.

Augustine establishes that suicide is a mortal sin because it rejects the grace of God. By using Judas as the epitome of evil, suicide was equated with all those who had been instrumental in the death of Christ. It therefore becomes heresy. In wishing to curb martyrdom Augustine had unwittingly established a precedent. Later Church law followed: a suicide as heretic cannot have Christian burial rites and this in turn abrogated property inheritance rights (Council of Orleans, 535); in 693 even attempted suicides were excommunicated (Council of Toledo). St Bruno called suicides or martyrs 'martyrs for Satan'.

But Augustine does not condemn *all* suicide. In the cases cited so far what he rejects is martyrdom for self-glory, or escape from persecution, i.e. egoistic suicide. At the end of his discussion he writes that some like Samson may have 'acted on divine instruction and not through human mistake – not in error, but obedience'. In other words Augustine, like Plato, accepts that in some cases self-killing is the mark of a very great person as a sign of their altruism and trust in God.

1   A man of compassion would be ready to excuse the emotions which led them to do this. Some refused to kill themselves, because they did not want to escape another's criminal act by misdeed of their own. Anyone who uses this charge against them will lay himself open to the
5   charge of foolishness. For it is clear that if no one has the private right to kill even a guilty man, then certainly anyone who kills himself is a murderer, and is the more guilty in killing himself the more innocent he is of the charge on which he has condemned himself to death. We rightly abominate the act of Judas, and the judgement of truth is that
10 when he hanged himself he did not atone for the guilt of his detestable betrayal but rather increased it, since he despaired of God's mercy and in a fit of self-destructive remorse left himself no chance of repentance.

Augustine, *The City of God*, 1:17–26

b) St Thomas Aquinas (1225–74)

Aquinas' *Summa Theologiae*, II.II. discusses suicide in the context of justice and **Natural Law** (NL). Aquinas develops the argument by christianising Aristotle's observation that man's existence is to be part of a community. Suicide is not only breaking God's law but a tacit rejection of the natural justice of society.

● Suicide is wrong because it is against Natural Law. NL suggests that our natural will is 'to love and cherish oneself'. It is therefore a 'fatal sin against nature'.
● It is injurious to society as a whole.
● It wrongs God. Life is a gift from God who ultimately has control of life and death.

The Augustinian/Aquinas argument still forms the heart of the official teaching of the Roman Catholic church today but the condemnation of the suicide to eternal punishment is modified with a better understanding of psychology. The *Catechism of the Catholic Church* states:

1   Grave psychological disturbance, anguish or grave fear of hardship, suffering or torture can diminish the responsibility of the one committing suicide. We should not despair of the eternal salvation of persons who have taken their own lives. By ways known to him alone,
5   God can provide the opportunity for salutary repentance. The Church prays for persons who have taken their own lives.

Catechism of the Catholic Church (1994), pp. 491–492

4 Psychological considerations

If Hume and other philosophers had liberated suicide from the religious and philosophical restrictions, the work of psychologists has given the moral philosopher important data by which to assess the motives of the suicide. For the past hundred years suicide has been regarded not as a deliberate act against society or God but a moment when the person had become confused and acted out of desperation. However, the conclusions from psychology do not necessarily confirm the conclusions of liberal philosophers. If anything psychologists suggest that suicide is the result of a distorted society. The fact is that philosophers treat suicide in terms of 'rights', 'liberties', 'justice' and so on. Alvarez, who attempted suicide himself and whose book *The Savage God* investigates the complexities of suicide, comments:

> The act is removed from the realm of damnation only at the price of being transformed into an interesting but purely intellectual problem beyond tragedy and morality.
>
> A. Alvarez, *The Savage God* (1974), p. 92

Alvarez finds in the writings of Sigmund **Freud** (1856–1939) a genuine attempt to understand the deeper motivations behind suicide. Freud's initial thesis had been based on the pleasure principle. The basic instinctive drives which determine a human's existence were primarily for survival and sex (libido). But the case of self-destruction led Freud to modify his initial thesis and make the following conclusions:

- In the case where a person has lost someone close to them the *ego* (self) tries to restore that person to itself. In the normal run of events the ego comes to realise that the dead person no longer exists in the external world but is now internally valued.
- In *'melancholic'* cases the person feels responsible as a killer for a loved one's death and attempts to atone through their own death and because the person 'lives on' in them they feel that they must avenge the death of a loved one.
- The **death instinct** or *thanatos* is an aggressive self-destructive drive to preserve the ego; in the case of the neurotic something as disturbing as a death or bereavement in childhood can be too strong for the ego to cope with.
- Suicide therefore is not strictly a means of escaping life but of purifying a deep-seated guilt.

The implications of Freud's analysis are far-reaching. It suggests that it is possible to have a culture of 'suicide' where deep-seated guilt is part of the psyche of that culture (look at Roman and early Christian culture). On the other hand it suggests that egoistic suicide is not really so much an act of free will as a delusion. There is an equally strong sense in which humans feel that a suicide is a wasted life and make every attempt to dissuade someone from taking their own life. Some care should be taken to contrast Hume's rational analysis with the more complex psychological response.

a) Contingent suicide and paternalism

So far we have considered suicide in terms of the egoist and the altruist. Psychologists try to explain the 'attempted' suicide cases which are more of a cry of despair than any true wish to self-kill. To this we can add one more category, called here **contingent suicide**, that is where a person undertakes a job or activity which has a very high chance of death – smoking, drug use, bomb disposal expert, miner and so on. All these types of suicide pose a difficult moral and legal problem concerning the extent to which we should interfere in a person's own best interests. Interference of this kind is termed **paternalism**. In a liberal society interference of the state should be minimal and only to such a degree as to allow maximum happiness. Inevitably paternalism seems to contradict the liberal premise which allows a person to choose their own destiny, but at the same time it aims to protect the individual from hasty and rash decisions and from the exploitation of others. The case of suicide presents just such a tension. A good example is the UK 1961 Suicide Act, where suicide is seen as the prerogative of the individual but must not involve others in the procurement of suicide. Part of the reasoning is to protect the individual from the exploitation of others. This issue is particularly acute in the case of euthaniasia (see Chapter 4).

Jonathan Glover establishes two 'guiding principles' (*Causing Death and Saving Lives*, 1977, p. 176):

● It is desirable where possible to save a worthwhile life.
● It is desirable where possible to respect a person's autonomy.

Glover acknowledges that in suicide cases it is very difficult to know how to apply these principles *consistently*. He wonders to what extent someone 'bent on suicide' should be talked out of it and whether this encroaches unduly on their autonomy. His solution is essentially pragmatic: if one does interfere and it works then a worthwhile life has been saved, if not 'the outcome is no worse than it would otherwise have been'. In the case of those who 'gamble with their lives' (to use Glover's phrase), that is those who knowingly undertake dangerous activities, the intervention of the law must be in proportion to the risks involved. Of course, Glover argues, no one wants an over-fussy or coercive state, 'but when the risks increase, the objections should diminish'.

Answering structured and essay questions

Summary

1 *Moral attitudes to suicide*: views from the past and attitudes today. Changing social attitudes.

2 *Philosophical arguments*:

a) Plato
b) Aristotle
c) Stoics
d) Christian

e) Hume
f) Kant
g) Existentialists

3. *Theological arguments*:

a) The Bible
b) Augustine

c) Aquinas
d) The Catholic Church today

4 *Psychological arguments*: Alvarez and Freud. The arguments so far have been intellectual and have not dealt with the state of mind of a suicidal person.

5 *Paternalism*: The difficult balance between allowing a person to decide (autonomy) their own life and interference from others. Glover; 1961 Suicide Act.

Questions

1a Explain why some philosophers and theologians consider suicide to be wrong.

1b 'It is not right to interfere with someone if they wish to commit suicide' Discuss.

2a Explain why Christian theology considers suicide to be a sin.

2b Discuss the types of suicide which you think are not blameworthy.

3 'Suicide is not immoral if there is no after life.' Assess this view with reference to at least two philosophers or theologians.

4 'A society which permits suicide has lost its moral grip.' Do you agree? Give reasons for your answer.

Essay skills

Note your reactions to the following situations. These can then be used later as examples in your essay.

Explain when you would/would not interfere and for what reasons:

● A married father of three offers to go on a highly dangerous mission behind enemy lines.
● A teenager threatens to take an overdose because of a failed love affair.

- Someone refuses to wear a safety belt in the car.
- A man wants to dive into an ice-cold river to save his dog.
- Socrates wishes to tell the truth, although he knows it will result in his death.
- You find your enemy with his head in the gas oven.

Explain whether you think the law should/should not interfere and for what reasons:

- Should the law intervene to ban boxing?

- Should mountaineering be limited to licensed mountaineers?

- Should smoking be illegal under the age of 21?

- Should the speed limit be abolished on the motorway?

The question of after-life is not dealt with specifically in this chapter. Augustine provides a good starting point because his ideas have been very influential in Western society. Consider his argument that suicide rejects God and allows no time for repentance so that damnation follows. By way of contrast you could look at the surprising conclusions of the atheist existentialists Sartre and Camus. Outline how suicide is the denial of freedom (it is 'bad faith'). Discuss what Camus means by the absurd. Alternatively you could look at Hume's atheistic argument and note how he rejects the notion that suicide is against God's laws. You must be clear what *immoral* means for each writer. You may wish to suggest that psychological research has made our judgements and made more compassionate.

'A society which permits suicide has lost its moral grip.' Do you agree? Give reasons for your answer.

The opening paragraph should consider whether morality is a public or private affair. The answer is complex. You could decide to opt for a liberal view where personal choice is significant or you may feel that a definition of society is one where we all have a concern for each other.

In the next part of the essay you may decide to analyse Hume's essay. Summarise his essay in sections and criticise. You might then contrast Hume's egoism with the non-religious views of Kant. Alternatively you may wish to contrast Hume with Christian thought. Both views argue that Hume has not taken society seriously enough.

You might then consider whether by permitting suicide (through legislation) the state is symbolically permitting some forms of killing (consider euthanasia, Chapter 4) and making a more brutal, less caring society. If society interferes then it shows its concern but also overrules personal autonomy. Does this matter?

3 Abortion and Infanticide

acts and omissions – a person can only be blamed or applauded for what they do

cognitive criterion – test for determining whether a human or foetus is a person. According to Locke's definition, a person is one who has the ability to be rationally reflective, has a sense of the past and future and can communicate

double effect (DDE) – where the primary intention to do good is accompanied by an unintended bad side-effect, the good intention legitimises the action

ectopic pregnancy – the embryo develops in the fallopian tubes rather than implanting in the womb – this could prove fatal to the mother

embryo – organism in the womb up to 9 weeks' gestation

ensoulment – the moment when the soul enters into the body. In traditional Christian thought, 40 days for boys and 90 days for girls

foetus – the organism in the womb from 9 weeks to birth

Hippocratic Oath – formulated in the fifth century BCE it became the basis for doctors' ethics, though now replaced by other promises. It stipulates specifically against abortion

infanticide – killing of a child outside the womb

ordinary and extraordinary means – in the Natural Law tradition, moral duties may be based on what would ordinarily apply to humans in all like situations. A patient may refuse certain forms of treatment on the grounds that they are 'extraordinary', i.e. over and above what is essential

pre-embryo – sometimes refers to the organism from conception to 14 days

speceist – discrimination against animals because they are considered to be intrinsically inferior to human beings

therapeutic abortion – abortion is permitted to protect the mother's health

viability – when the foetus is considered able to sustain its own life, given reasonable care

1 The politics of human life

> **KEY ISSUE** Nowhere is ethical discussion more complex and
> more heated than in questions concerning life and death. The
> key issue is what constitutes a person and what rights and
> liberties are afforded to that person.

We know how inconsistent we can be. A little girl stuck down a
disused mine shaft in Wales can capture the attention of a whole
nation and entail the mobilisation and cost of the rescue services. But
an earthquake in another part of the world where thousands are
dying does not necessarily mean that we abandon the rescue of the
girl and put the money towards saving a village of hundreds. This
case and many like it suggest that we do not have a consistent attitude
to the value and sanctity of human lives. But there is more to it than
this: there is also a political agenda.

The issue of abortion is particularly important because it
highlights a state of confusion within Western morality. The abortion
issue is as much a political debate as a moral one. This is particularly
so in the USA where the anti-abortionist or **pro-life** movement is
associated with right-wing evangelical or traditional Christianity and
old-fashioned values. The **pro-choice** movement represents modern
liberal democracy with its emphasis on, and some would say
absolutising of, personal autonomy. We need to consider whether the
values derived from the Judaeo-Christian tradition are still
sustainable in a complex world of sophisticated medicine, shifting
attitudes to religion and assumptions of personal autonomy and
rights.

The following imaginary case is from a famous article by Judith
Jarvis **Thomson** ('A Defence of Abortion', 1971). The analogy
illustrates in the first instance the kind of moral values we assume
independently from abortion. What makes Thomson's argument
significant is that she argues for abortion even though the foetus
might be considered a person.

1   But now let me ask you to imagine this. You wake up in the morning
    and find yourself back in bed with an unconscious violinist. He has been
    found to have a fatal kidney ailment, and the Society of Music Lovers
    has canvassed all the available medical records and found that you
5   alone have the right blood type to help. They have therefore kidnapped
    you, and last night the violinist's circulatory system was plugged into
    yours, so that your kidneys can be used to extract poisons from his
    blood as well as your own. The director of the hospital now tells you,
    'Look, we're sorry, the Society of Music Lovers did this to you – we
10 would never have permitted it if we had known. But still, they did it, and
    the violinist now is plugged into you. To unplug him would be to kill

him. But never mind, it's only for nine months. By then he will have recovered from his ailment, and can safely be unplugged from you.' Is it morally incumbent on you to accede to this situation?

'A Defence of Abortion' in P Singer (ed.), *Applied Ethics* (1986), p. 38–39

The story raises the following particular moral issues:

- What rights, if any, does the violinist have over 'your body'?
- What minimal duties do 'you' have to the violinist?
- How would 'you' justify unplugging the violinist from your circulatory system?
- What difference, if any, does it make to 'your' decision that the violinist is presently unconscious?
- Do the conclusions above suggest that a woman has a right to terminate an unplanned or unwanted pregnancy?

Abortion, though, raises some very basic moral questions:

- Is all human life intrinsically worthwhile?
- Is all direct killing of humans (i.e. intentional killing) always wrong?
- Is it always a duty to preserve innocent human life?
- Are personal autonomy and happiness less important than duty to others?

2 Sanctity and quality of life arguments

There is a growing opinion that to none of the above questions can the answer always be a categorical or unequivocal yes. For those such as Peter Singer (*Rethinking Life and Death*, 1995) all these questions rest on an outmoded sanctity of life argument which fails to represent what people *actually* think and do. Singer argues that:

- In practice those who hold a SOL position only make it workable by smuggling in quality of life (QOL) arguments (see Chapter 1, page 5, Kuhse). That is, they argue on grounds (for example) of compassion that if a life is so miserable then the kindest thing to do is to 'let it die'. So whenever SOL arguments make use of **acts and omissions**, or **ordinary and extraordinary means**, or the **double effect**, they are trying by philosophical sleight of hand to get round an unworkable doctrine (see page 44).
- The SOL is **speceist** – in other words it assumes that only *human* life is intrinsically worthwhile. But if the criteria which determine the sacredness of the developing human **foetus** in the womb were to be applied more generally then there would be no grounds for killing animals for food or experimentation. As it is, the SOL is arbitrary, discriminatory and **androcentric** (sees all values only in human terms).
- Being a person is not automatically associated with being human. Not all humans are persons and not all persons are human. Being a person is associated with having a sense of time, a future and self-awareness, yet

recent studies show that chimpanzees display more of these characteristics than a newly-born human baby. Duties to actual persons can only be in relationship to those who express their preferences through conscious behaviour. The foetus is not automatically a person nor does it necessarily have the rights associated with being a person.

For Singer and others like him, abortion is not an evil. However, Singer's case often rests on an unsubtle rendering of the SOL and an assumption that any variation of the SOL is an implicit affirmation of his secular QOL. He acknowledges himself that his views on handicapped children and **infanticide** will shock many and even those who tacitly implement QOL criteria find that his form of utilitarianism is too cold and detached to be entirely workable.

a) Human foetuses/babies as actual persons

Both SOL and QOL arguments argue that humans as persons should be treated as moral agents with all the rights and considerations which society gives to persons. The argument, though, begs the question: when do humans become persons and become part of the moral community?

i) Ensoulment
Historically the Christian church used as its scientific basis the Aristotelian tradition that **ensoulment** or the moment when God breathed the spirit into the foetus took place 40 days after conception for boys and 90 days for girls. The tradition became orthodoxy through Aquinas although clearly it lacked biological knowledge. Aquinas distinguished various stages in which the foetus developed: the 'vegetative soul', then the 'animal soul' and finally the 'human soul'. The judgement was probably made loosely on the moment when the foetus **quickened** or moved in the womb. However in the seventeenth century, with better biological knowledge, the Church adopted the view that life begins at conception. This has remained the standard view in most Christian churches, therefore abortion was tantamount to murder. John Calvin's (1509–64) view expressed here is representative of both Protestant and Roman Catholic churches.

> The foetus, though enclosed in the womb of its mother, is already a human being. If it seems more horrible to kill a man in a house than in a field, it ought surely to be deemed more atrocious to destroy a foetus in the womb before it has come to light.
>
> John Calvin, *Commentary on the Last Four Books of Moses*

ii) Conception

Conception is the moment when the sperm penetrates the outer membrane of the ovum (woman's egg) and unites its genetic material with the genetic material of the ovum's nucleus. The attractiveness of this view is that it marks a definite moment when the human being comes into existence. Unlike other claims, body and soul form a psychosomatic whole and there is no single moment when the separate soul enters the cells of the body. Genetically what is now created could only be *Homo sapiens* and if that is so it has a human life.

> Human life must be respected and protected absolutely from the moment of conception. From the first moment of his existence a human being must be recognised as having the rights of a person – among which is the inviolable right of every innocent being to life.
>
> *Catechism of the Catholic Church* (1994)

iii) Syngamy

Those who object to the conception boundary do so because becoming a person is a process and not an exact moment. Syngamy is the process lasting for some 24 hours from the penetration of the ovum by the sperm to the conjoining of the two sets of genetic material. In other words fertilisation is from the beginning a *process* and if that is so, conception is not in itself necessarily a unique, specific moment. Even so, the Society for the Protection of Unborn Children or SPUC (*Love Your Unborn Neighbour*, 1994, p. 96) argue that this has trivialised the 'irreversible events which determine which of many possible human beings comes into existence'. This is the moment when the sperm penetrates the ovum membrane.

iv) Implantation

Implantation (six days to a week) is the moment when the cluster of cells or *morula* travels from the fallopian tubes (where it has developed from sperm and ovum) to implant in the lining of womb. It is only at this stage that there is more than a 60 per cent chance of the foetus developing to a full-term baby. The likelihood up to this stage is around 30 per cent. For some reason it becomes the morally symbolic moment when the foetus forms a relationship with the mother as a person. The Roman Catholic theologian Bernard Häring comments:

> I feel that the argument ... is an overstatement of the case if it asserts that implantation is the definitive moment of the ontogenesis of the human person.
>
> *Medical Ethics* (1991), p. 76

v) Pre-embryo

Given that conception is a process, some consider that for the next 14 days what is developing is not life or a person. It is only after this stage that the individual emerges when the cells split and **monozygotic twins** emerge. This, it is argued, is the first moment when the cells can truly be considered individuals and not just a collection of cells.

But Glover sees no objection. Conception could be considered the time when 'at least' one person emerges (*Causing Death and Saving Lives*, 1977, p. 123), and SPUC concludes 'if one body can become two, we should therefore have no difficulty in accepting that one soul can become two' (*Love Your Unborn Neighbour*, 1994, p. 98). The **Warnock Committee** (whose recommendations became the basis for the 1990 Human Fertilisation and Embryology Act) chose the fourteenth day to distinguish the individual human **embryo** from its **pre-embryo** state and to permit the use of embryos up to this stage to be used for experimentation and research. But the argument is peculiar. Although the committee used the fourteenth day as the moment when an individual foetus can be discerned at the primitive streak stage, the moral argument rested on the rather arbitrary claim that the embryo is only really important because the mother *feels* it so. What happens to the status of the foetus whose life is not considered important?

vi) Brain activity

The attractiveness of selecting brain activity as the start of life is not only that it uses the **cognitive criterion** as the start of life but that it can also be used as the criterion to determine the end of life (in brain-stem dead cases or persistent vegetative states). The problem here is whether brain activity has to be continuous or whether life begins at the first spasmodic moment. Spasmodic brain activity occurs at 54 days, EEG (or electroencephalography, which registers different types of brain waves) activity at 14 weeks and continuous brain function at 32 weeks. Less certain is whether this activity is in any sense conscious. Some take it in the minimal sense that it marks the first phase in consciousness (much like Aquinas' vegetative and animal soul). Sporadic brain activity may be considered to be no more or less than when a person falls into a coma and then recovers or falls into a deep sleep then awakes. We would not say that they are less of a person whilst in these states. Others, on the other hand, argue that the foetus can only be considered a person at the end of the process with the completion of the cerebral cortex. It is only then that the foetus is able to have a continuous spiritual existence (see Häring, *Medical Ethics*, 1991, p. 79).

vii) Viability

From the twenty-second day onwards the heart of the foetus begins to beat and by day 42 the foetus is recognisably a human baby measuring 23–23.5 mm. As we have seen, brain function and cell appearance are poor indicators of whether the foetus is alive in the way we would call human. An ancient criterion is that of **viability** or the ability to be independent. As noted above, this used to be considered the time when the baby 'quickened' or moved, today it is considered by some to be the moment when the baby is sufficiently well developed to live outside the womb.

Abortion legislation in many countries often sets an upper limit based on the principle of viability (in the UK 24 weeks) for cases where there is no abnormal foetal development. But such a limit is not an absolute boundary. Many argue that the law would be better leaving the decision of viability to the doctors. They claim that the tendency is to treat the upper limit as the definitive moment and that the foetus can only be viable *after* this time. Furthermore, as medicine improves so the chances of giving a premature baby (even at 18 weeks) the ability to live become increasingly probable. Even so, many are disturbed by the possibility that a baby delivered at 22 weeks could be considered either a premature birth or a late abortion. The choice is whether to allow one to die or the other to live.

viii) Birth

Legislation in many countries allows abortion up to the moment of birth (usually in exceptional circumstances) but regards the deliberate killing of the baby after birth as murder. As we have seen, clear boundaries are very difficult to determine so why should birth be any different? But some suggest that birth does mark a psychologically new moment. Mary Anne Warren, for instance, argues that birth is the moment when the baby no longer depends on the mother and has become the concern of the wider community. The mother is no longer the one absolutely necessary factor for the child's survival. But supposing the child is rejected (for whatever reasons) by the mother and the wider community, what are the moral grounds which govern infanticide?

Michael Tooley and more recently Peter Singer argue that the developmental process of the child is still so limited at this stage by any reasonable definition of what a person is (see page 4, where Singer adopts Locke's view) that many animals such as chimpanzees display *more* developed characteristics of being a person than the new-born human. On these grounds infanticide will, of course, be wrong to those who would *prefer* the child not to die. But as the child itself displays no particular preferences whether to live or die (especially in severely handicapped cases) then direct and intentional killing of babies is not an intrinsic wrong (see page 45 for further discussion).

Table I Abortions in England and Wales, 1996	
Weeks of pregnancy	**Number of abortions**
under 9 weeks	69,926
9–12 weeks	85,083
13–16 weeks	14,779
17–20 weeks	5,266
21–24 weeks	2,078
25 weeks and over	92
not stated	1

Source: Office for National Monitor AB 97/4 (July 1997)

b) Human foetuses/babies as potential persons

The quest to find clearly determined boundaries is notoriously difficult.

- Boundaries usually mark thresholds rather than clear moments which occur in the development of the foetus. Thresholds are necessary mostly for legislative reasons.
- The notion of 'person' is a broad term and contingent on whether one adopts one or more of the following viewpoints: a religious view (which includes the notion of a soul); a mechanistic view (which includes some account of the brain's development); a social-biological view (which includes some account of the individual's relationship in the community).

One solution is to consider the foetus as a **potential person**. The foetus can be considered at whatever stage as a human being who will (all things being equal) develop into a person. An abortion is always wrong as it will cut short a life which might have another Mozart, or a great scientist or charismatic statesman, for example. As discussed in Chapter 1 (page 3) we often lament the death of a child because we feel that its life has been 'cut short' and that he or she will be unable to enjoy whatever potential talents they may have had. The Christian SOL states that no human may cut short (innocent) life because that is the divine prerogative of God (see Job 1:21 and also Chapter 1, page 11). The attractiveness of the potential person position is that it avoids the difficulty of deciding when to assign a soul to a clump of cells or a full-blown personality at birth. If we take Dworkin's view (Chapter 1, page 3) that life as *bios* is really an account much like a story where the potentials at each stage contribute to the next, then it might be possible to avoid difficult speculation about when the foetus/baby has a soul, or desires or develops conscious preferences.

The arguments against the foetus/baby as potential person include the following:

● Is the present value of the foetus/baby only to be judged by what it *might* be? I can't arrest a window-shopper because I think he or she might become a shop-lifter. An abortion is therefore not directly killing an actual person if I am claiming that the foetus is only a potential person. It is often for reasons like this that many pro-life groups reject the potential person argument:

> Personhood in the sense of 'the state of being a person' admits no degrees.
>
> SPUC, *Love Your Unborn Neighbour* (1994), p. 43

● For some it is a slippery slope to killing any human being whom one regards as being only a potential person but not a full or actual person. The results of the Holocaust where such a principle was enacted on a huge scale make us very wary about using such ideas and language.

● Some argue that if the principle of contraception is accepted as a means of family planning as well as the potential person arguments then abortion become morally acceptable. When it takes place is arbitrary. Let us assume that by potential life we mean the moment at conception when the potentials first come into being. But if this were the case then it might be claimed that the sperm and egg also have potential to create life and it would be equally wrong wilfully to destroy them if there was the opportunity to realise their potentials. (If for instance a couple choose this month rather than next to have a baby does it mean that in other months a particular egg's potential has been wasted?) If contraception is part of a selection procedure, then might not abortion be seen as an extension of choosing to give this foetus an opportunity to realise its potentials rather than another?

● Finally there is a problem of consistency. Would those couples who adopted the potential person view be obliged to produce children whenever possible and to avoid contraception? (For a fuller argument read Glover, *Causing Death and Saving Lives*, 1977, pp. 122, 138–40.) Such a view is endorsed in the Roman Catholic teaching on contraception and the family, although it does not go quite as far as to suggest that contraception is direct killing.

3 From hard cases to personal autonomy

Both the pro-choice and the pro-life groups have as their premise that *'every child is a wanted child'*. Both agree that there is nothing worse than bringing a child into the world who is unwanted, unloved or rejected. But after that initial agreement the extremes of each viewpoint diverge with no possibility of agreement. The vitalist (pro-life) *a priori* is that all life is wanted so no direct abortion is possible whereas the extreme pro-choice *a priori* leaves all decisions with the woman as the owner of her womb.

However, the debate is not as polarised as some suggest. It is possible to hold a SOL viewpoint where abortion in some circumstances is possible without advocating a quality of life viewpoint as such (despite Singer and Kuhse's accusation of being closet QOL supporters). Situations where abortion is considered to be acceptable will be determined by current attitudes to the foetus/baby as person set out above. The situations below begin with so-called hard cases where even those who hold pro-life views might consider these exceptions. These include: rape/incest, handicap, and threats to the mother's life (**therapeutic abortion**). The second category is where abortion is often considered to be a personal affair and primarily a woman's health care matter. These include: family planning, threats to mental states and any threats to personal autonomy.

a) Rape

It was the rape by British soldiers of a young girl in 1938 which justified Dr Aleck Bourne carrying out an illegal abortion in order to safeguard her mental health. At the trial he was acquitted. The precedent established grounds for abortion as an exception and eventually became the basis of the UK 1967 Abortion Act. In the famous case of *Roe v. Wade* (USA, 1973), 'Roe' or Norma McCorvey claimed she had been gang-raped and, suffering from suicidal feelings, requested an abortion. The decision of the Supreme Court of the USA to allow the abortion effectively liberalised all US federal abortion laws. What are the moral grounds that justify abortion in these cases? The primary consideration is the traumatic circumstances in which conception takes place.

- The QOL which employs a broadly utilitarian/consequentialist basis has to determine whether an unwanted pregnancy of this kind will not only continue the trauma for the mother but also for her existing family. Furthermore it might be argued that any child of rape might also suffer the trauma of learning of their violent origins. Dealing with a rape in its early days where it is believed that the development of the foetus is not yet an actual person presents fewer problems in the equation. But given that rape is a horrendous experience and it might well take some time for the woman to seek advice, by this time the pregnancy has progressed. What are the moral problems for those who consider the foetus to be an actual person?
- The Church of England's report (*Abortion: an Ethical Discussion*, 1965), for instance, adopts a view very close to Singer's preference utilitarianism. The arguments rests on a weak SOL (See Chapter 1, page 13) where the life of a child has to be considered within the context of the family. Rape

is not a trivial issue and to insist that a woman must have a child falls outside the primary Christian context of love. Abortion is not without its own pain and those who pursue it consider it as an act of sacrificial love.

● Alternatively the question can be considered in terms of violation of rights and reduction of autonomy. Judith Jarvis Thomson's argument ('A Defence of Abortion', 1971) justified a woman who is pregnant through rape (or unplanned pregnancy) having an abortion primarily on the grounds of ownership rights over her body. Thomson outlines the following connected justifications:

- *self-defence*: the strain on the woman's body warrants 'direct killing' of an innocent party;
- *ownership*: it is her body, in the same way that we might say it is her house or it is her life; she has a *prior* claim to her body and so she can remove the foetus whenever she wants to;
- *priority of rights*: the possible rights of the foetus are acknowledged, but seen always to be less than hers, because it is *using* her; the right is only possible if she chooses to acknowledge it as a right. She may on the other hand choose to ignore it;
- *consent*: the foetus can have no right to claim her unless she has consented fully;
- *minimal good/responsibility*: there is no law which compels us or her to be good Samaritans especially at our own expense. The woman might wish to help the foetus but the sacrifice is too much.

But in all these justifications which consider the foetus as a person the objection is that the foetus is still being killed directly or indirectly. The objections to rape as a legitimate ground for abortion include:

● In almost every consideration above, abortion was justified in terms of the mental health of the mother. In other words it was no more than her preference not to continue with the pregnancy. For many this is the *slippery slope* where all exceptions lead, which they fear will result in *abortion on demand*.

● It is very difficult to imagine a case where one would be justified in expelling an innocent person from one's *property* if this resulted in death. Furthermore, the argument is distasteful to some feminist writers who object to the depersonalising of the woman's body as 'property'.

● Abortion as a form of *self-defence* assumes that the foetus has evil intentions. Rape *may* result in a life-threatening situation, but the foetus itself does not have malevolent intentions. If anyone is to blame, it is the rapist not the foetus.

● Whilst it may be acknowledged that the foetus cannot have the same *rights* as a fully grown and responsible adult and also that a woman cannot be expected to rear the child unless she wishes to, her rights do not include the right to kill an innocent child. She may have to carry the child for some time but it can then be passed on for adoption at birth or earlier through extraction.

● *Consequential* arguments fail to take into account the psychological damage that abortion can cause. Some argue that although the short-term consequences of an abortion may help, the ensuing guilt caused by killing the baby adds to the initial trauma of the rape. The evidence here is difficult to assess on both sides – there are those who claim that abortion reduces the pain of rape. SPUC, for instance, argues from the Christian perspective that by having the child good may come out of bad through a woman's 'courageous and generous commitment to life' (*Love Your Unborn Neighbour*, 1994, p. 58).

b) Handicap

The question of handicap has already been briefly referred to (see page 35 above). Singer makes the issue of handicap one of the lynchpins of his QOL argument. He chooses as his example the important USA case of **Baby Doe** (1982), the Down's syndrome baby whose parents allowed him to die after advice given by the hospital obstetrician Dr Owen (see Singer, *Rethinking Life and Death*, 1994, pp. 106–15). The case caused huge interest and a series of 'Baby Doe rules' appeared which attempted to prohibit withdrawing treatment from handicapped babies.

Singer focuses on Dr C Everett **Koop**, the US Surgeon General, and ardent upholder of the SOL who, as one who had done considerable work with handicapped children, was chosen by the Reagan administration to champion the pro-life argument. However, although he judged that Down's syndrome babies should always be treated, he was prepared in extreme cases (i.e. a child without a brain or no intestine) to allow babies to die. In these cases his judgements are justified by judging them on the basis of *ordinary* not *extraordinary* means. In other words if the treatment of a severely handicapped person should fail to improve their condition then doctors would be justified in giving only the kind of medical treatment which a healthy child would receive. But Singer is unimpressed. Ordinary and extraordinary means beg all kinds of questions and are really no more than another way of stating what Koop must have already assessed – the future quality of life which the baby might expect. Singer cites the following quotation as evidence that Koop did not hold a SOL but a QOL argument. Koop said of a child born without an intestine:

1 We would consider customary care in the case of that child the provision of a bed, of food by mouth, knowing that it was not going to be nutritious, but not just shutting off the care of that child, nor do we intend to say that this child should be carried on intravenous fluids for
5 the rest of its life.

quoted in P. Singer, *Rethinking Life and Death* (1994), p. 110

The case illustrates the enormous problem of deciding what constitutes 'handicap' and whether a life is worth living. The key issue (as it was debated in the various amendments to the Baby Doe rules) is the value or preference parents place on the baby when given the medical prognosis of their child. Dr Owen, who had advised the parents of Baby Doe, said he was 'proud to have stood up for what I and a large percentage of people feel is right'. His advice, in utilitarian terms, had minimised the suffering of the parents, enabling them to have another healthy baby, which would not have been possible had they been tied to looking after Baby Doe.

Dr Owen's medical advice about the capabilities of Down's syndrome babies was later severely criticised, but nonetheless standard medical advice during pregnancy is often in contradiction to this criticism. Many pregnant women undergo as a matter of course amniocentesis tests which show if the foetus has a chromosome abnormality (e.g. in the cases of spina bifida or Down's syndrome). In almost every case abortion is recommended as standard practice. Singer argues that the gap between infanticide and abortion on the grounds of handicap is narrowing. The UK Human Fertilisation and Embryology Act (1990), for instance, permits abortion at any stage on the grounds of foetal abnormality. In other words, there is already an accepted implicit view that some human beings are of less *value* than others. Singer goes further. By comparing some handicapped humans to more developed animals, we will come to realise that our speceist and androcentric views will have to be adjusted. In short, not all humans have a *right* to life. In time the abortion/infanticide distinction will have to disappear:

1   When we do that, however, we will not be able to avoid noticing that, if we set the standard anywhere above the bare possession of life itself, some human beings will fail to meet it. Then it will become very difficult to continue to maintain that these humans have a right to life, while
5   simultaneously denying the same right to animals with equal or superior characteristics and capacities.

P. Singer, *Rethinking Life and Death* (1994), p. 183

In 1996 out of 177,225 abortions there were 1943 in England and Wales recorded as having been due to a 'substantial risk of serious disability of child'. The arguments against abortion of the handicapped clearly have implications for the treatment of the new-born even allowing that birth sets up a new relationship between child, mother and society.

One of the most significant features of the infanticide debate to emerge in recent times is to what extent the baby is the sole concern of the mother (or parents). For instance the US Americans with Disabilities Act (1992) protects those with a wide range of disabilities from discrimination. It has also been applied to new-born babies. In other words, the decision whether a child should live or die is not the sole prerogative of parent or doctor. It is deemed to be a *public* affair. So, if as Singer and others suggest, there is no major moral distinction between pregnancy and birth it follows that there is no *automatic* reason to abort a handicapped child in the womb. If the law can give rights of protection outside the womb, then it follows that it can extend these rights to the womb.

Perhaps reactions to handicap are more to do with fear of being in that position oneself; a fear of being locked into a body whilst retaining all one's present experiences and wishes. It would be like saying to someone who had not been able to go to university because they were simply not intelligent enough that they must be living a miserable life. There need not be any direct correlation between intelligence and happiness. Down's syndrome people manage IQs of 30–70, sufficient to live a life (i.e. in Dworkin's terms, life as '*bios*') with a history and in their own terms to respond socially given sufficient love and care. Gregory Pence concludes:

> To put it another way, they will have a narrative history, and their lives can go better or worse for them. To put it another way, most of them would *not* be better off not existing … consequently, the best interest of these babies is served by maximal treatment.

> *Classic Cases in Medical Ethics* (1995), p. 191

Of course, as Dr Koop argued, there are times when in extreme cases the doctor feels that the degree of handicap is such that even extraordinary treatment would be fruitless. This does not license direct killing, even though 'ordinary means' might in the end result in death. Abortion as a form of direct killing, on these grounds, could not be justified.

Finally, there is the broad principle which underpins the SOL, which is that all human life should be treated with care and love. It is the basis for medicine and enshrined in the older doctors' ethic, the **Hippocratic Oath**, not wilfully to kill. Christian ethics looks to the example of Christ whose life and teaching particularly singled out the weak, the ill, and the marginalised as examples of those whom the Kingdom of God welcomed. Compassion as a Christian principle means to 'suffer with' and it warns against treating others as things or objects. Kant's secular version puts it very simply: never to treat people as a means to an end but as an end in themselves. Thus the care for the handicapped is not a question of preference but one which accepts life, in whatever form, as part of the human condition.

c) Threats to the mother's life

Until the middle of the twentieth century, the only grounds for abortion were when a pregnancy threatened a mother's life. Even back in the sixteenth century Thomas Sanchez argued that an embryo could be aborted in an **ectopic pregnancy** (i.e. where the embryo has not implanted in the womb but is continuing to develop in the fallopian tubes). He used as the basis for his argument Augustine's just war argument, where reasonable force might be used to defend oneself against a life-threatening aggressor. The argument in a secular form has already been referred to in Thomson's article (in Singer, 1986) which argues for the mother's right to use force against physical threats to protect her own interests.

However, both these arguments fail to take into account the innocence of the embryo or foetus. In the Natural Law tradition it is immoral deliberately and directly to will the death of an innocent person. Abortion may be justified using the **double-effect** (DDE) principle. It is possible to imagine a situation where everything possible has been done to save the mother and baby's lives, but where, in giving attention to the mother's health, the side-effects of medical treatment have *indirectly* (and so unintentionally) resulted in the death of the baby. Even pro-life organisations such as SPUC allow for DDE, although they are careful not to advertise it. The following passage is the only time in their book that killing a 'baby' is openly permitted:

> The removal of tubal ectopic pregnancy is not generally regarded as an abortion procedure since the *primary* intention is to protect the mother's life, not to destroy her unborn child.
>
> *Love Your Unborn Neighbour* (1994), p. 48

The criticism, as always with the DDE, is a question of true intentions. It is impossible to gauge these and critics of the DDE argue that any good doctor will know the likely effects of treatment, so the DDE is a piece of 'sophistry' (clever argument) to keep the SOL intact.

Criticisms of the threat to life argument include the following:

● The DDE doesn't adequately settle the *value* of mother and baby. If both lives are deemed to be equally valuable according to the SOL, might we not choose to treat the baby and not the mother? It is of course possible to imagine this. There are indeed very rare cases where the mother has known that in saving her child she will die as a result.

● The alternative is to risk losing both mother and baby rather than permit the deliberate killing of mother or baby. Such a paradoxical view is deemed by WSOL (weak sanctity of life) to be contrary to the principle of Christian compassion.

● Many pro-life groups cite cases where physical threats to lives are replaced, in a slippery slope, by psychological threats. The *Roe* v. *Wade* case is an example where the mother threatened suicide if the pregnancy continued. Once this principle is permitted as an exception (as it is in the 1967 Abortion Act), then anything which is deemed to threaten the life of the mother becomes grounds for abortion. As evidence for this they point to the present state of affairs where liberalising laws in Europe and the USA, at first for threats to lives, have now resulted in abortion for reasons as weak as 'threats to my career', 'threats to my freedom'. Statistics (see Table 2) illustrate that the vast majority of cases are not life-threatening.

Table 2 Number of abortions in England and Wales for each of the statutory grounds, 1996	
A: Risk to mother's life	138
B: To prevent grave permanent injury to mother	2,471
C: Risk to mother's physical or mental health	171,175
D: Risk to existing (born) children's health	12,227
E: Substantial risk of serious disability of child	1,943
F: In emergency – to save mother's life	3
G: In emergency – to prevent grave permanent injury to mother	0
Total (doctors sometimes cite more than one category for reasons for abortion)	177,225

Source: Office for National Monitor AB 97/4 (July 1997)

d) Personal choice

In all the above cases the assumption has been that the grounds for abortion are exceptions to the rule that life should be preserved. There are also good utilitarian grounds for dissuading a mother from a late abortion where it might have adverse physical and mental repercussions. However, given the variety of opinion as to when the foetus can be considered a person with rights, and the impossibility of deciding whether a person's motives are genuine, what moral grounds are there for prohibiting early abortions?

● **The Liberal Principle:** We discussed earlier the possible anomaly between late abortions on grounds of handicap and allowing handicapped babies to die. One distinction made was that birth marks the moment when the baby is considered to be independent from the mother and governed by public laws. The question is whether it should be the moment of birth which is the determining factor of viability. The shift in law is to see viability as the significant moment and to apply Mill's liberal principle. The principle (see Chapter 1, page 7) avoids the 'tyranny of the state' and intrusion into what is essentially a private moral affair. In other words whatever moral outrage others may feel, this cannot restrict the autonomy of the individual to do whatever he feels is right. It is therefore not just a female rights issue, but more generally, that a citizen may adopt any religious, moral or political stance in private.
● **Abortion on demand:** The state still has a duty to serve the best interests of its citizens. In practice abortion laws in many countries

impose some stipulations in order to protect the individual from hasty or dangerous procedures. Anti-abortion groups might reasonably ask that women be aware of what the process of abortion entails and to consider its possible physical and psychological side-effects.

● **Abortion as contraception:** As we have seen, Thomson gives a strong argument for abortion after rape; could this also work for the case where contraception has failed? Could it be argued that the unexpected intrusion of the foetus into the woman's womb justifies its protection? But Thomson does not envisage abortion being used as an *alternative* to contraception; carelessness or negligence cannot be defended by appealing to self-defence or priority of rights. However, a woman who uses contraception as a means of controlling her sexual freedom and autonomy may well see abortion as a continuation of the same process. In practice this seems now to be the case (see Table 1). In the 1996 abortion statistics for England and Wales, for those women aged between 14 and 49 abortion was 13 per 1000 women, the highest being among women aged 16 to 19 (25 per cent) and those aged 20 to 24 (27.2 per cent).

4 History and law on abortion

The history of abortion until the early part of the twentieth century is almost entirely determined by the Judaeo-Christian tradition. The legal injunctions in the Old Testament on abortion see it primarily in terms of loss of property. Exodus 21:22–25 for instance distinguishes between deliberate and accidental hitting and killing of a man and the accidental hitting of a pregnant woman causing her to miscarry. Although the punishment is explicit that deliberate killing is a capital offence, the passage is less clear about miscarriage and seems to treat it as loss of property liable to a fine. There are many passages dealing with the sanctity of life even in the womb (see theological considerations below). Infanticide as sacrifice is especially repellant (see Genesis 22).

The New Testament is silent on the subject. Medieval law was influenced by attitudes to sexuality based on Augustine's view that sex was primarily for procreation of children and Aquinas' notion that the foetus becomes a person at ensoulment. Punishment for abortion was therefore determined by the stage of the pregnancy and condemned at the stage where the foetus received its human soul (i.e. at 40 days for boys and 90 for girls). This flexible view of abortion can be seen in seventeenth-century European common law, where abortion even at 'quickening' was not always an indictable offence, although in 1803 an English statute (Lord Ellenborough's Act) made abortion after quickening a capital offence. However, during the nineteenth century the Roman Catholic Church in its response to new biological advances finally settled on conception rather than quickening and dispensed with the distinction between formed and unformed infants. Pius IX allowed 'abortion' only on the principle of double effect for extreme cases of ectopic pregnancy and uterine cancer. The development of abortion laws in the nineteenth century formed part of Victorian reforms in welfare, medicine and sanitation.

a) Development of the law in the UK and USA

- 1861 *Offences Against the Person Act:* those who killed the baby in the womb could be punished with a maximum sentence of penal servitude for life.
- 1929 *Infant Life (Preservation) Act:* protected the child in the womb at any time *capable of being born alive* and at least from 28 weeks onwards. It also protected the child during birth and immediately afterwards. Abortion or 'induced birth' was permitted only in cases where the mother's life was endangered.
- 1938 *Rex v. Bourne:* Found in favour of Dr Bourne's abortion of a 14-year-old girl who had been raped on grounds that her mental health would have been affected through giving birth.
- 1967 *Abortion Act:* The law intended to clarify the 'exceptions'. Its intention was to deal with hard or borderline cases. The Act permits abortion on the grounds that the birth of the child would cause mental and/or physical suffering to the mother and/or existing children, or if the child would suffer great handicap. The aim of the Act was to exonerate the doctor from prosecution if two doctors could give their assent on at least one of the six grounds for abortion outlined in the Act.
- 1990 *Human Fertilisation and Embryology Act:* The Act was the result of the Warnock Committee's report on the use of donors, surrogates and *in vitro* fertilisation. In the process of determining when fertilised embryos might be used in experimentation the Act redefined the exceptions of the 1967 Abortion Act and effectively abrogated the 1929 Act (only in England and Wales) with its upper limit on abortion now set at 24 weeks. More importantly it allowed abortions *any time up to birth* in cases of grave threat to the mother's life and handicap of the foetus.
- USA, 1973 *Roe v. Wade:* From 1965 the Supreme Court had already agreed to personal liberty in the use of contraception and the same principle was upheld in this case. However the rights of the woman had to be weighed against the rights of the foetus. For legal reasons viability (when the foetus is 'potentially able to live outside the womb' i.e. 28 weeks) was drawn as a line after which states could if they wished make abortion illegal. The law divides pregnancy into trimesters: a) judgement left to the physician attending the pregnant woman, b) the state may regulate the pregnancy 'reasonably related to the maternal health', c) the state may 'proscribe abortion' except for the 'preservation of the life or health of the mother'.

Table 3 Grounds for Abortion under the 1967 Abortion Act and amended under section 37 of the Human Fertilisation and Embryology Act 1990

A The continuance of the pregnancy would involve risk to the life of the pregnant woman greater than if the pregnancy were terminated.

B The termination is necessary to prevent grave permanent injury to the physical or mental health of the pregnant woman.

*C The continuation of the pregnancy would involve risk, greater than if the pregnancy were terminated, of injury to the physical or mental health of the pregnant woman.

*D The continuance of the pregnancy would involve risk, greater than if the pregnancy were terminated, of injury to the physical or mental health of any existing child(ren) of the family of the pregnant woman.

E There is substantial risk that if the child were born it would suffer from such physical or mental abnormalities as to be seriously handicapped.

Or in an emergency:

F To save the life of the pregnant woman; or

G To prevent grave permanent injury to the physical or mental health of the pregnant woman.

*Grounds C and D may take place up to 24 weeks. All other grounds are without time limit.

Two doctors must give their assent to permit a doctor to carry out the abortion.

A conscience clause permits a doctor to refuse to be involved with an abortion (see BMA, *Rights and Responsibilities of Doctors*, page 70).

---

5 Theological considerations

Throughout the discussion above the place of the Christian Churches has been fundamental in the history and present debate about abortion. There is, though, no consensus because even adherence to a sanctity of life principle begs questions about when life begins and, in difficult situations, whose life requires the greater portion of Christian compassion and care. For the sake of clarity we shall group the theological responses into three broad areas.

a) Anti-abortion

As we have seen above, the **Roman Catholic Church** has for a considerable time opposed abortion, based on the Natural Law tradition that innocent life from conception must be preserved. The statement is classically outlined in the encyclical *Humanae Vitae* (1968). Some discussion surrounds the use of the double effect (DDE) to justify 'abortions' or 'indirect abortions' in life-threatening circumstances. But the anti-abortion standpoint is not the sole province of the Roman Catholic Church. Conservative or evangelical Christians who base their ethics primarily on the authority of the Bible conclude that the Bible extends the command to 'love one's neighbour' to the child in the womb and from conception. This follows a strong SOL (see Chapter 1, pages 10–11) that humans are made in the image of God (Genesis 1:27), that murder is a capital offence (Genesis 9:6), that only God can give and take away life (Job 1:21), that given difficult situations one must 'choose life' (Deuteronomy 30:19–20) and Christ's life and death were so that Christians 'might have life and have it abundantly' (John 10:10). More problematic is determining what the Bible has to say about when life begins and more specifically about abortion. Conservative interpretation of Exodus 21:21–25 distinguishes between hitting a woman and causing her to miscarry the baby alive (punished with a fine) and treats verse 23 'if any harm follows, then you shall give life for life' to refer to the death of the child as a heinous crime. This is confirmed by other passages where abortion and infanticide are treated as pagan and immoral acts (see 2 Kings 15:16 or Amos 1:13 for instance).

A large number of biblical texts suggest that the child in the womb should be considered as a person. The psalmist in Psalm 139:13–16 writes 'you knit me together in my mother's womb' and Job 10:18–19 and Jeremiah 20:16–18 both speak of wishing to return to the security of their mother's womb rather than see the sorrow and suffering of the world. Finally the New Testament regards the incarnation of God in the person of Jesus to be at the moment of conception in Mary's womb (Luke 1:15). That Jesus and John the Baptist are both regarded as persons in the womb is recorded in Luke 1:41–44 when John *in utero* 'leaps' in his mother Elizabeth's womb with joy when he recognises the infant Jesus in Mary's womb. Objections to this line of thinking are outlined below. Equally important in Christian ethics is the flexibility to cope with special circumstances and the avoidance of the Pharisaic practice of making moral law more important than the spiritual welfare of individuals.

b) Abortion in exceptional circumstances

The line taken by many Christian traditions such as the Church of England and Methodist Churches is that abortion should be permitted only in rare cases where there is threat to the mother's mental or physical health. The Church of England's report in 1965

Abortion: An Ethical Discussion, provides a theological background to the 1967 Abortion Act. Theologically this tradition gives overriding compassion to the needs of the mother (by following the weak version of the SOL). More recent publications maintain the Church's position but there is increasing and widespread concern that abortion is not being used as an exception but as a form of contraception. The Abortion Act is perceived in many ways to have failed to solve a wider social problem.

The following statement by the Church of England's Board of Social Responsibility was made in response to the Roman Catholic Archbishops of Great Britain in 1980. The Church of England has no official position, but the statement represents its current thinking.

1　In the light of our conviction that the foetus has a right to live and develop as a member of the human family, we see abortion, the termination of that life by the act of man, as a great moral evil. We do not believe that the right to life, as a right pertaining to persons, admits
5　of no exceptions whatever; but the right of the innocent to life admits surely of few exceptions indeed. Circumstances exist where the character or location of the pregnancy renders the foetus a serious threat to the life or health of the mother, in such circumstances (and they are extremely few and well-known) the foetus could be regarded
10　as an 'aggressor' on the mother. The mother would be entitled to seek protection against the threat to her life and health which the foetal life represented. If in those circumstances a choice had to be made between the life of the mother and the continuation of the pregnancy, precedence should be given to the mother's interests; but such a
15　choice would only arise if no less drastic remedy for the ill existed. The undoubted evil of abortion would in this situation represent the lesser of two evils, only resorted to as the appropriate way of caring for the mother if the evil of a significant threat to her life or health cannot otherwise be avoided ...
20　A proper concern for the law should not blind us to the fact that it has at best only a limited and indirect role in protecting the true interests of persons and of the community. The request for abortion is frequently a pointer to underlying personal or social problems, which cannot be dealt with by a law on abortion, however framed. It cannot
25　solve the problems of the girl who needs to prove herself by becoming pregnant, nor those of the tired mother facing an addition to an already overlarge family in poor housing. Nor can it help a society which is in turmoil in its attitude to human sexuality, free of earlier fears but unable or unwilling to accept the unconditional commitment and
30　creativity which sexuality essentially points to, enables, and requires. We as Christians are aware that it is quite inadequate to limit ourselves to expressions of moral disapproval of the individual women who seek and obtain abortion on what often appear quite inadequate grounds.

Our moral concern for the *protection* of human life will only have and
35 be seen to have integrity if it also finds expression in an equal concern
for whatever *enhances* human life, and also for whatever *undermines* it.

Abortion and the Church (1993), pp. 27–8

c) Situationism

The most radical development in theological thinking mirrors the
kind of preference utilitarianism promoted by Singer and others.
Since the 1960s many Christian theologians have argued that Jesus'
teaching was not to legislate but to give people their own freedom to
act responsibly based on the principle of generous love or **agape**
which wills our neighbour's good (e.g. see Luke 10:30–37). Joseph
Fletcher's influential book *Situation Ethics* (1966) coined the term
situationism and set out a Christian calculus (much like Bentham's
hedonic calculus) which decides each case on its own merits. Fletcher
outlines a case in 1962 where an unmarried, schizophrenic girl was
raped by an inmate of the mental hospital where both lived. However,
her father's request for an abortion was denied because the only
moral and legal grounds for abortion would have been if her life was
in grave risk. Fletcher finds it shocking that this kind of rigid legalism
could deny compassionate treatment through the claim that
maintaining the moral laws of the Church allows God to bring about
the best outcome. There is no law which tells one specifically what to
do. The situationist answer cannot be predicted because each case is
unique but in the case of the raped girl Fletcher argues that her
mental health is paramount and furthermore 'no *unwanted and
unintended* baby should ever be born'. Situationism is criticised for
the same kind of shortcomings which utilitarianism suffers from and,
as the passage below illustrates, Fletcher is far from clear about why
and to what extent the embryo or foetus should be included in the
calculus:

1 They [situationists] would in all likelihood favor abortion for the sake
of the patient's physical and mental health, not only if it were needed
to save her life. It is even likely they would favor abortion for the sake
of the victim's self respect or reputation or happiness or simply on the
5 ground that *no unwanted and unintended* baby should ever be born.
    They would, one hopes, reason that it is *not* killing because there is
no person or human life in an embryo at an early stage of pregnancy
(Aristotle and St Thomas held that opinion), or even if it *were* killing, it
would not be murder because it is self-defense against, in this case, not
10 one but *two* aggressors. First there is the rapist, who being insane was
morally and legally innocent, and then there is the 'innocent' embryo
which is continuing the ravisher's original aggression! Even self-defense

legalism would have allowed the girl to kill her attacker, no matter that he was innocent in the forum of conscience because of his madness.

15 The embryo is not more innocent, no less an aggressor or unwelcome invader! Is not the most loving thing possible (the right thing) in this case a responsible decision to terminate the pregnancy?

Situation Ethics (1966), p. 39

Answering structural and essay questions

Summary

1 *Politics of abortion:* The present debate is between traditional and liberal values. This has become a political issue. Thomson's example of the violinist illustrates to what extent we are free to choose our own future and our responsibility to others.

2 When do foetuses become actual people? When are they entitled to rights of protection? The problem of deciding at what stage a foetus is a person.

   a) Ensoulment
   b) Conception
   c) Syngamy
   d) Implantation
   e) Pre-embryo
   f) Brain activity
   g) Viability
   h) Birth

The argument can also be considered from the point of view of the foetus as a potential person.

i) Potential persons: Do potential-person arguments rule out the use of contraception? What are the weaknesses of this view?

3 *From hard cases to personal autonomy:* Which extreme cases might permit the use of abortion? How far is personal autonomy significant?

   a) rape: *Roe v. Wade* case, self-defence, ownership, rights, consent and responsibility;
   b) handicap: Baby Doe case. American and British law;
   c) threats to mother's life: double effect, slippery slope arguments;
   d) personal choice: woman's right, abortion on demand, as contraception.

4 *History and Law: important laws* – 1929, 1969, 1967, 1990 (UK), 1973 (USA).

5 *Theological considerations:*

   a) anti-abortion, pro-life arguments;
   b) exceptions: Church of England and Methodist views;
   c) situationism: liberal Christian viewpoint, Fletcher.

Questions

1a Explain why the issue of abortion is a major political issue for some people.
1b Assess the view that abortion is always morally wrong.
2a Explain in what circumstances abortion is considered to be the lesser of two evils.
2b 'Abortion is a private moral decision and the law should make it available on demand'. Discuss.
3 'Deciding when human life begins is primarily a moral not a biological issue.' Discuss.
4 Outline and assess the theological grounds for the termination of a pregnancy as a consequence of rape.
5 What, if any, are the moral distinctions between abortion and infanticide?
6 Does a human embryo/foetus have an absolute right to life?

Essay skills

Essays on abortion are popular amongst candidates. Examiners will want to ask questions which test those who have thought about the specific ethical issues and principles of abortion – not just the broad questions about whether it is right or not. It is important that you consider the philosophical and theological principles. Be clear that there is no one view amongst doctors, Christian thinkers or philosophers. There is considerable diversity of opinion, for instance, on whether the double effect works as an idea. Try to form your own opinions on these matters. Avoid discussion about the methods of abortion – by and large these are irrelevant. You cannot and should not include everything in one essay. Be selective of the material; argue and evaluate as you develop your position.

'Deciding when human life begins is primarily a moral not a biological issue.' Discuss.
This is a question about what it means to be a person. You must try to give a brief working definition of what it means to be a person (see Chapter 1). The question can be taken at a straightforward level to consider whether life begins at conception, for instance, or the first brain waves (be selective of your material here). You might wish to argue that life 'emerges' and that it is impossible to give a 'moment when' argument. If so, what are the moral implications? If birth is significant because the baby becomes a member of the moral community then the argument is based on a moral evaluation and not just a biological one. What are the implications of this? Evaluate (refer to specific philosophers or theologians) and then conclude by referring back to the essay title.

4 Euthanasia and Doctors' Ethics

1 Good or bad medical practice?

KEY ISSUE   Euthanasia or 'a good death' is distinguished from suicide in that it involves in some way the direct or indirect use of a third party.

A 'third party' in law refers to any agent other than the principal agent and in the case of euthanasia this would generally mean a doctor (sometimes also referred to as the 'physician'). For all practical purposes if euthanasia is to be justified at all it has to be considered as part of medical practice, for it is reasonably clear that any other practice of euthanasia would be almost impossible to control or regulate. Without regulation society would permit killing or murder and whatever moral code one adopts would be regarded as untenable. The consideration of 'euthanasia', at present, is rightly a medical issue. Put simply it is this: should a doctor kill his patients in some circumstances?

Consider the following hypothetical cases from the point of view of a doctor:

- *Case 1*: Mrs White is 36 years old, and has decided that she wishes to die. She asks you, because you are knowledgeable in drugs, for a prescription so that she can administer a fatal dose in the least painful way possible. She is not suffering from any mental or physical illness as far as you know.
- *Case 2*: Alfred is 86 years old and suffering from incurable cancer. He asks you to leave him an extra quantity of painkillers when you leave. This is an unusual request and you suspect that he intends to take an overdose so as to kill himself.
- *Case 3*: Rachel, 18, is suffering from leukaemia. She has asked to die. The doctor refuses but you administer the maximum appropriate chemotherapy and drugs to allay the cancer. The doctor knows that every dose will probably shorten her life.
- *Case 4*: David, 27, has suffered a terrible car accident which has left him permanently paralysed from the neck downwards. He has asked not to have any extra help other than the usual food and liquids. He has refused to have any extra treatment such as dialysis. Without such treatment he will die.
- *Case 5*: An elderly man, with no relatives, is on a life-support machine and whilst he is on it he can live for a good many years. He has promised you a substantial amount of money in his will when he dies. One day, whilst leaning over to help the man the nurse accidentally, and without noticing, pulls out an important tube. You refrain from doing anything.
- Case 6: Susan, 41, two months ago had a massive brain haemorrhage and although her body still functions with the aid of life-support, doctors have declared her brain-stem dead.

None of these cases is entirely the same. Which if any would permit the use of euthanasia? More importantly, does a doctor think that deliberately cutting short a life, however ill, or even at the request of his patient, is good medicine? The official position of the British Medical Association, for instance, suggests that there is a great deal of difference between actively terminating life and treating a patient in a manner which may in the end result in death.

1   In its ethical advice the BMA emphasises that it is the duty of a doctor
    to ensure that a patient dies with dignity and as little suffering as
    possible but recommends that active intervention to terminate life –
    that is, where drugs are given or other procedures carried out in order
5   to cause death – even at the request of a patient, should remain illegal.

The Rights and Responsibilities of Doctors (1992), p. 77

a) Moral crisis in liberal societies

Why does the issue of euthanasia (and abortion) cause such heated
debate at present? Peter Singer has argued (1994) that Western
liberal societies are going through a transitional stage in ethics at
present where the authority of the traditional 'Sanctity of Life'
argument (SOL) is giving way to the liberal 'Quality of Life'
argument (QOL). The liberal influence has already been seen in
many acts of legislation, notably in the case of suicide (see Chapter 3
for a fuller argument), where the principle of personal autonomy is
the fundamental principle underpinning moral and legal decisions.
Singer suggests that the SOL belongs to an older more absolute value
view of life (see Chapter 1) but with the demise of Christianity the
philosophical basis which establishes life as a gift from God or part of
a Natural Law can no longer be sensibly sustained. So, while the
changeover takes place there will be those who strenuously wish to
oppose what they see as a corrosive force. Whilst Singer's argument
may have much to commend it we should also bear in mind that the
SOL as much as the QOL argument both have to contend with the
increasing technological and medical complexity. Whereas in the
past pneumonia was considered to be the old person's friend or a
severely brain-damaged child would have died through natural
causes, the doctor now has the means to sustain a life which in the
past simply would not have been a possibility. Whilst the moral basis
for sustaining life and allowing death is in transition, the medical
profession and legislators will continue to inspire strong reactions.

b) Three moral principles

Three principles presuppose that the doctor is working from the
traditional SOL position enshrined in the part of the Hippocratic
Oath which states 'I will give no deadly medicines to anyone if asked,
nor suggest any such counsel' (BMA *Handbook*, p. 69). Each of these
principles depends on making a distinction between *direct* and
indirect killing, i.e. **active euthanasia** or **passive euthanasia**. In the
latter case there is some dispute whether the term 'euthanasia' is
really appropriate.

i) Acts and omissions

If A chooses to shoot B then we classify this as an intended act; if C sees A and fails to stop A shooting B then this is an intended omission. The point is whether C is at all blameworthy. In this incident, if C is a pacifist they might well justify their action by appealing to a negative responsibility, i.e. by failing to act they were morally blameless. They might even argue that refraining from acting took a great deal of moral courage. But however one looks at it, C was prepared to condone the death of B and accept whatever consequences this might entail. Some object to this. Can I be held responsible for failing to help stop the deaths of thousands dying in poverty in the Third World? Perhaps the notion has to be couched in such terms as 'I am only responsible when I am reasonably in a position to do something'. In other words some 'omissions' are regarded as 'acts' (see page 78 for further discussion on capital punishment). The Roman Catholic Church states:

1 Thus an act or omission which, of itself or by intention, causes death in order to eliminate suffering constitutes a murder gravely contrary to the dignity of the human person and to the respect due to the living God, his Creator. The error of judgement into which one can fall in
5 good faith does not change the nature of this murderous act, which must always be forbidden and excluded.

Catechism of the Catholic Church (1994), p. 491

The problem is particularly acute with premature babies. If a baby is born very prematurely a doctor might have to consider whether they have a duty to save the baby. Some argue that morally they may *withhold* treatment either as a form of passive euthanasia (a form of **non-voluntary euthanasia**) or simply 'letting nature take its course'. Morally if they engage in treatment and *then* decide to *withdraw* treatment on the grounds that the baby will no longer have a worthwhile life, it may no longer be considered indirect killing but an act of active non-voluntary euthanasia or murder. (See Singer, *Rethinking Life and Death*, 1994, pp. 75–80 for examples and discussion.)

ii) Double effect

Another *indirect* argument has a long tradition in Natural Law ethics and involves two kinds of intention. According to the double effect (DDE) argument there is a difference between foreseeing an event and directly intending or *willing* it to happen. The emphasis, therefore, is different from the act and omissions argument where the agent foresaw what was to happen and allowed it to happen. For instance, A defend themselves against an attack from B using reasonable force. They know that this *might* result in B's death but it is not their intention that this should happen. If B then dies as a result of A's defence the DDE does not hold A to be blameworthy for an act they did not intend. In Case 3 a doctor who subscribes to the DDE might argue that the principle is sound medicine (and as a well-established principle in Natural Law ethics it is therefore acceptable in Roman Catholic theology). However, the term 'euthanasia' is resisted in the same way that 'abortion' is avoided for similar reasons (see page 47). But is the DDE open to abuse?

For instance:

- In the example of Case 3 above, those who criticise the DDE question how one can gauge a sound intention.
- Is there a satisfactory distinction between intending and foreseeing? Might one say that the DDE is *bad* medicine, that if I foresee death but fail to act, then this is an omission which is a form of indirect euthanasia – which is rejected by the SOL?

iii) Ordinary and extraordinary means

The principle of ordinary and extraordinary means is used both by weak SOL (WSOL) arguments and QOL proponents. Another, possibly better way of considering the issue is in terms of *proportionate* and *disproportionate* means.

- In the Natural Law tradition a person who refuses food and water in order to die has deliberately committed suicide which is condemned in Roman Catholic theology as a mortal sin (see page 26). But a person is within their rights to refuse surgery on grounds that it is over and above what is needed ordinarily for bare existence. The BMA for instance say, 'competent patients have a right to refuse any treatment, including life-prolonging treatment' (*Medical Ethics Today*, 1993, p. 149). Nature is allowed to take its course. The doctor is not involved in the *direct* cause of death of the patient. Those who criticise this suggest it is a form of passive euthanasia or even assisted suicide. For instance, if a doctor withholds life-sustaining treatment, against his or her better judgement, but through respect for patient autonomy, the result might be condemned either as an act of professional negligence or wilful killing.
- On the other hand, some argue that it is a doctor's professional duty to use whatever medicines are available regardless of the situation. A response to this might be to think in terms of *proportion* as an alternative variation of extraordinary means. Proportion is a well-established principle in the Natural Law tradition which may be applied to medicine without compromising the obligation of the doctor to treat his or her patient. This enables each situation to be seen individually so that what might be considered proportionate to achieve good ends is contingent on the needs of the patient and even the *resources* of the doctor. The issue is particularly complex with non-competent patients. For instance, a very handicapped baby (for example one who is 'anacephalic' or with a major part of the brain missing) might be considered so ill that no amount of surgery would improve

their condition significantly. In this case a doctor might then prescribe 'nursing care only' (the baby should be kept warm and fed) as proportionate to their needs, knowing that the baby will die shortly.

● The WSOL (see page 13) argues that where death is inevitable the doctor is bound by *compassion* or love to treat the patient accordingly. This attitude is summarised by the much quoted phrase, from Arthur Clough's poem: 'Thou shalt not kill; but need'st not strive Officiously to keep alive'. Singer (*Rethinking Life and Death*, 1994, p.149) goes further. Rigid adherence to the doctrine never to kill (vitalism) is an abrogation of the doctor's responsibility to his patient. The question is not so much between ordinary and extraordinary means but whether, in some cases, direct termination of life is good medicine.

● In QOL the key factor is whether the use of extraordinary medical means would usefully promote the quality of life. The notion is essentially utilitarian. For instance, in Cases 4 and 6 above a number of factors all need consideration: the possible length of useful life; state of mind of the patient (a main consideration in the American **QALYS** or Quality Adjusted Life Year Schedules); resources needed and available. All these factors contribute towards making doctors' choices. For instance a doctor might have to weigh up whether very painful surgery or powerful drugs which cause permanent drowsiness would result in a person who is a shadow of their former self. Can he or she base his or her judgement on some minimum human life-standard? For instance John Finnis's 'basic goods' argument suggests a possible list of 'valuable' life criteria which include: play, aesthetic experience, sociability; but inevitably there is no agreement as to what these standards should be.

c) The doctor–patient relationship

The essence of the Hippocratic oath was to establish the right kind of doctor–patient relationship. In the past the role of the doctor tended to be paternalistic. The doctor as professional upholder of the sanctity of life told the patient what to do. The shift in emphasis in recent years has been to acknowledge the rights and autonomy of the patient. The doctor's role has developed accordingly to guide and inform the patient and, in the final instance, to comply with the patient's wishes. The issue of euthanasia in this area is complicated because it involves a decision which cannot be reversed and may either depend on a confused or frightened patient, or a patient who is unable to express their wishes. In these cases a doctor or physician has to make hard choices. This can be analysed by considering the different types of euthanasia:

i) Voluntary euthanasia

Now that the legal objections to suicide have been set aside in most countries it follows that 'assisted suicide' should be possible. Those organisations who argue for it stress that it is now established that to take one's own life as an example of personal autonomy is a protected right in a liberal society. The Voluntary Euthanasia Society argues that:

- 'Physician aid in dying' enables a person's death to be a 'good death' with dignity rather than a bungled and degrading one (and so better than **physician-assisted suicide**).
- Once a person has the knowledge that they can die *when* they wish it this often give them the courage to live fuller and longer lives.
- Many doctors feel that assisted suicide at the request of their patients is good medicine. A survey in 1985 (NOP for the Voluntary Euthanasia Society of Scotland) suggested that 45 per cent of doctors questioned would consider administering a lethal injection.

Those who argue against this on the grounds that this weakens the patient–doctor relationship raise the following range of objections:

- Assisted suicide is the 'ultimate abrogation of personal responsibility' (Brown, *Choices*, 1983, p. 130) on the part of the patient.
- Real care for the sick and dying is to be found in a caring environment. The hospice movement (whether Christian or secular) allows a person to die in dignity and in a loving environment. David Brown suggests there is a great deal of difference between 'letting go' and 'cutting off' (*Choices*, p. 127). Likewise the BMA makes clear that whereas *treatment* by doctors may vary from patient to patient, and there can be severe cases where to prolong life would be 'unacceptable', however when treatment is withdrawn 'care must always continue until the very end of the patient's life' (*Medical Ethics Today*, 1993, p, 159).
- Old people especially might worry and indeed fear that their doctor will want to suggest euthanasia as good medicine. They might feel it is their duty to request euthanasia as they are a *burden* to others. Euthanasia would very quickly lose its voluntary nature.
- Doctors' relationships with their patients are always those of hope; the inclusion of the possibility of euthanasia puts an intolerable burden on them. Euthanasia is contrary to their training as a doctor where the principle of beneficence is the process of pain relief not harm. The option for a doctor to kill their patient (even on request) might be too easy and remove their duty to find suitable pain management (*Medical Ethics Today*, 1993, p. 154).

ii) Involuntary euthanasia
Involuntary euthanasia places the burden of responsibility on the doctor. In this case the situation is where the patient is unable to communicate meaningfully or coherently his or her wishes but where it is imagined that if the patient were lucid he or she would ask to die. In this case the doctor may consult the wishes of the patient's relatives

or friends or a nominated proxy or in some cases (where the patient has previously made his intention plain) through an **advance directive** or living will (although the legality of these is still under debate in many countries including the UK). An advance directive, written whilst the person is competent, could set out what health care treatment or non-treatment should be administered if a patient should become incapacitated, or how decisions should be taken, In some countries a person carries a 'do not resuscitate' form similar to an organ donor card. A proxy continues, albeit imperfectly, the doctor–patient relationship. Objections include:

- A situation when reached might be very different from the one envisaged when making an advance directive.
- The 'proxy' may be in a very emotional state and unable to represent the patient's wishes calmly.

iii) Non-voluntary euthanasia

Inevitable the cases where non-voluntary euthanasia might be realistically employed are extreme. The means are frequently passive or indirect and involve the *withdrawing* of care rather than direct killing. In non-voluntary euthanasia a decision is made on behalf of the patient on the strength of the situation. The landmark case of Tony **Bland** in the UK was after the Hillsborough football disaster in April 1989. Bland was placed on life-support and although able to feed and breathe was in a deep coma. Finally after lengthy legal debate his life-support was turned off. The significance of the case is that it acknowledged that doctors cannot be expected to maintain a life (however defined) at all costs. The moral issue is whether prolonging life of 'brain dead' patients is in their best interests.

d) PVS, death and the patient's best interests

The Bland case and others like it have set up a precedent which has significantly shifted not only how we understand death but the value of life as well. In the past death was defined when the heart ceased pumping blood round the body accompanied with the cessation of other vital bodily functions. Today, a person can be kept 'alive' in this sense for very great periods of time even though, as in the Bland case, important parts of the brain have ceased to operate. Being 'pink and supple' does not necessarily equate with being alive. Coma patients in this state can perform a number of involuntary actions and, contrary to what many people perceive, the patient is not necessarily lying inert in bed. The new definition of death is when there is no brain activity. So, a patient who is in a **PVS** (persistent vegetative state) where they have lost part of the brain (i.e. the cerebral cortex) would theoretically be deemed dead even if his body was functioning. But recent research has revealed how difficult making such a diagnosis is. Not only can it take some time to determine whether the patient is indeed brain dead but it is now apparent that the brain can function at a very low level, just enough to provide hormones for the body (see Singer, *Rethinking Life and Death*, 1994, pp. 35–7).

In practice being in a PVS or being declared 'brain dead' is not always taken to mean that the patient is dead (if that were the case then there would be no debate). The issue in broad terms is whether sustaining the patient on life-support is in the patient's best interests. In other words, 'life' is not just a biological fact but also a *moral* or evaluative judgement. In the end each case has to be viewed separately. The BMA concludes: 'The ability to make complex judgements about benefit requires compassion, experience and an appreciation of the patient's viewpoint' (*Medical Ethics Today*, 1993, p. 170). The following represent the conclusions of those who propose a QOL basis for non-voluntary euthanasia.

- The key issue is whether the patient displays any kind of characteristics which indicate consciousness. Without the ability to express wishes or preferences the quality of life is deemed to be sufficiently low as to justify withdrawal of treatment.
- Preferences should include the views of family or proxies as well as medical staff. In practice many hospitals now have 'ethical committees'.
- Biological existence is not enough to determine the quality of a life.

But there are those who argue that if the patient is physically capable of sustaining a life, then the termination of life, however poor quality, is wrong. For instance they argue that:

- if doctors can consider being able to transfer healthy organs from the person who is in PVS then that person is still a viable human being and must be allowed to live;
- all humans are equally valuable and judgements made by doctors and family about the quality of life are never in the 'best interests' of the patient;
- it is wrong to cause the death of an innocent human being whether he or she is unconscious or not;
- non-voluntary euthanasia of PVS patients is murder.

2 Law and morality

KEY ISSUE   The issue of euthanasia raises the thorny problem of the relationship between law and morality. Does the law make something right? Is it always right to obey the law?

So far the discussion has centred on the doctor–patient relationship within the constraints of law. There is no doubt that a shift in public opinion has increased the pressure for reform especially for voluntary euthanasia, whilst the Bland case sets a precedent for severely brain-damaged patients.

a) The liberal model

Mill's essay *On Liberty* (1859) is often cited as an example of the way in which law should function in a liberal society.

- The principle is that law *is not in itself* a moral guideline. Law in a liberal society acknowledges that each person has his or her own preferences which, using the utilitarian principle, if satisfied lead to the greatest happiness. The law enables the greatest personal autonomy of the greatest number.
- The second function of law is to protect the individual. This limits the majority from exploiting the minority and also the minority from exercising too much sway over the majority. Law should have minimal interference.

In practice, though, the law has to take into account a general moral feeling and it has also to acknowledge that once legislation takes place, in the mind of many this is seen to give tacit approval to certain forms of behaviour. Bernard Williams has described this as the *precedent effect* (Smart and Williams, *Utilitarianism*, 1973, p. 106). Others more fearfully think in terms of a slippery slope or the thin end of the wedge. If, for instance, voluntary euthanasia were to be permitted under the law this would inevitably permit other forms of illicit killing. The British Medical Association is adamant that euthanasia should not become law:

> Doctors have a duty to try to provide patients with a peaceful and dignified death with minimal suffering, but the BMA considers it contrary to the doctor's role deliberately to kill patients, even at their request. In the BMA's view, liberalising the law on euthanasia would herald a serious and incalculable change in the ethos of medicine.
>
> *Medical Ethics Today* (1993), pp. 175, 177

b) The case for legalising euthanasia

The two principles frequently cited are personal autonomy (and rights) and QOL. The argument is further enhanced by citing those countries/states where some form of euthanasia is permitted.

i) Britain

Euthanasia is only an extension of what is permissible as suicide. The 1961 Suicide Act in the UK for instance permits personal autonomy to choose without recrimination (in the case of attempted suicide) but forbids third-party involvement. Here is an argument typical of this kind of reasoning (Janet Radcliffe, the *Guardian Weekly*, September 1992):

1   The problem with voluntary euthanasia has nothing to do with the dangers of letting doctors decide whether patients live or die … The real question is quite different. It is whether people who are trapped in bodies or an institution they cannot control should be allowed to make
5   choices freely available to the rest of us … Why? … If you take a housebound friend shopping no one accuses you of kidnapping; if you cook her a meal no one thinks you are force-feeding her. Why then, if she is in agony or despair, and you bring her the lethal dose she desperately wants but cannot get, or you manipulate the syringe
10 because she is too weak to do it herself, do you find yourself guilty of one of the worst of crimes there is?

But the 1961 Suicide Act makes it illegal to aid or give assistance in a suicide. Those who argue for a change in the law cite the shift in popular support and demand for voluntary euthanasia from 51 per cent in 1969, 69 per cent in 1976, 75 per cent in 1989 to 82 per cent in 1996. The British Medical Association though still strongly opposes any change on the grounds that it will irrevocably alter the patient–doctor relationship.

ii) The Netherlands

Often people argue that voluntary euthanasia arrangements should be brought in line with the principles determining legal abortion. The situation in the Netherlands is frequently referred to because it most clearly expresses the balance between the popular will, medical practice and legal control. (For a full account see Singer, *Rethinking Life and Death*, 1994, pp. 143–7). The case is for physician-assisted suicide.

● Mercy killing is illegal, but where there is a *conflict of duties* between the doctor's medical ethics and the demands of the patient euthanasia may be permitted. (The key issue therefore is that of conflict of duties.)
● Only a medical practitioner may be permitted to carry out euthanasia.
● The patient must make his or her request to die persistently and explicitly.
● The patient's request must be freely made, well informed and without coercion.
● The patient's condition must be one where there is no foreseeable room for improvement and where there is unbearable pain. All other alternatives for relieving pain should have been considered.

● A doctor should seek the advice and second opinion of another independent doctor.
● The Dutch parliament regularised this procedure in 1993. The doctor must report his or her action to the public prosecutor who then judges each situation case by case. A doctor may be prosecuted if the above criteria have not been adhered to.

iii) The USA
In the USA the movement is towards 'proxy empowerment' and developing the use of living wills. The movement is towards physician-assisted suicide. Physician-assisted suicide is strongly resisted by the pro-life movement.

iv) Australia
In Australia there is no uniform law; however, a doctor may discontinue life-support at the request of the patient. This does not constitute, for the purposes of law, assisted suicide. In the State of Victoria an act of 1988 permits a person to appoint a proxy. In South Australia a person may use an advance directive under the 1983 Natural Death Act refusing 'extraordinary treatments' should they become incapacitated.

c) Objections to legalising euthanasia
One of the primary objections to legalising euthanasia has been the slippery slope or wedge argument. The wedge argument is based on a form of logic which argues that what may be permitted initially as an *exception becomes the rule*. This is borne out by the observation that:

● there are always those who exploit a weaker rule
● what begins with the best of intentions results in undesirable ends.

Not surprisingly the wedge argument is supported by those who wish to uphold the SOL, those who have a strong deontology (that rules must be obeyed) and genuinely fear that exceptions are not in the end in people's best interests. The BMA cites (*Medical Ethics Today*, p. 153) the situation in the Netherlands where some 1000 (or 0.8 per cent) of all deaths a year are the result of non-voluntary euthanasia.

Helga Kuhse challenges proponents of the wedge argument to provide empirical evidence to support their case. Her own conclusion is that the wedge argument is used by scaremongers to support their complete ban on all forms of euthanasia. The most frequently cited example of the wedge argument is the active non-voluntary euthanasia practised by the Nazis during the Holocaust years as a form of *eugenics* (literally 'the production of good off-spring') where the deaths of millions were justified as part of the improvement of society. Kuhse concludes:

1   Whilst the Nazi 'euthanasia' programme is often cited as an example
of what can happen when a society acknowledges that some lives are
not worthy to be lived, the motivation behind these killings was neither
mercy nor respect for autonomy; it was, rather, racial prejudice and the
5   belief that the racial purity of the *Volk* required the elimination of
certain individuals and groups. As already noted, in the Netherlands a
'social experiment' with active voluntary euthanasia is currently in
progress. As yet there is no evidence that this has sent Dutch society
10 down a slippery slope.

'Euthanasia', in P Singer (ed.), *Companion to Ethics* (1991), p. 302

The SOL deontological response is to point to a number of recent
liberalisations in the law which illustrate the wedge taking effect. For
instance, abortion in the UK is illegal but is permitted in extreme
cases. Since 1967 (when the Abortion Act was introduced in England
and Wales), the large number of abortions for 16–24-year-olds
suggests that 'exceptions' (e.g. threat to psychological life of the
mother) are effectively being used as a form of birth control. Many
people now think that abortion is legal and in practice an abortion is
usually given on demand. Another example might be the liberalising
of the divorce laws and the decline of the family.

Finally, as we have already seen, there are those who argue that
legalising euthanasia would not promote patient autonomy but in fact
reduce it. Legislation would do irreparable harm to doctor–patient
relationships and destroy the trust which is essential if a doctor is
going to be able to administer the right kind of care. The following
extract from the British Medical Association illustrates the point:

1   We have consistently emphasised the importance of patient autonomy
and rights, reflecting the weight society assigns to individual freedom of
choice. Supporters of a right to die often present this issue as one of
personal liberty, maintaining that therefore individuals should be
5   entitled to assistance to end their lives at the time and in the manner
they choose. The BMA, however, maintains that autonomy has limits.
The rights of one group cannot be permitted to undermine the rights
of others. Recognising a legal right to die would have implications for
the whole of society and, perhaps, most particularly for its vulnerable
10 members.

    Thus many doctors fear that even a limited change in legislation
would bring about a profound change in society's attitude to
euthanasia. By removing legal barriers to the previously 'unthinkable'
and permitting people to be killed, society would open up new
15 possibilities of action and thus engender a frame of mind whereby
some individuals might well feel bound to explore fully the extent of
these new options. Once previously prohibited action becomes
allowed, the argument goes, it may also come to be seen as desirable
– if not by oneself, then as something which might be recommended
20 for others.

A social environment which recognised the right to die, we argue, would bring about a fundamental shift in social attitudes to death, illness, old age and disablement. It would encourage the labelling of people by group and result in some groups who presented problems
25 being seen as more expendable. It would also change the public view of the profession in an irrevocable way and undermine the trust that patients have in doctors.

Medical Ethics Today (1993), p. 151

Answering structured and essay questions

Summary

The following diagram indicates the kinds of choices and moral principles involved from the perspective of the doctor–patient relationship.

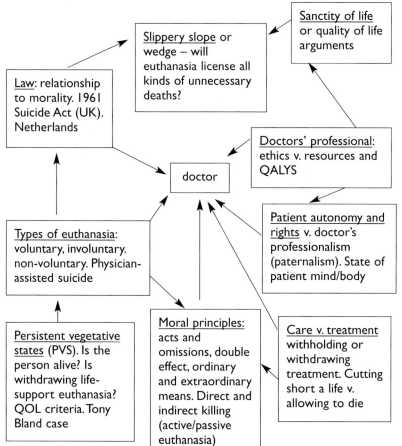

I   *Good or bad moral practice*:
   a) liberal societies: the clash between QOL and SOL, technology, life support, medicine;
   b) moral principles: Hippocratic oath, acts and omissions, double effect, ordinary and extraordinary means;
   c) doctor–patient relationship: voluntary euthanasia, involuntary euthanasia and non-voluntary euthanasia (include notes on hospices, treatment and care, beneficence, advance directive, withdrawing care);
   d) persistent vegetative state (PVS): patient, doctor and family relationships.

2   *Law and Morality:* the liberal principle (Mill):
   a) the case for legalising euthanasia: Netherlands, USA, Australia;
   b) the case against legalising euthanasia: the precedent effect and slippery slope/wedge arguments, Kuhse's response, patient autonomy.

Questions

1a Explain the moral arguments which makes assisted suicide different from voluntary euthanasia.

1b 'Euthanasia and suicide are two aspects of the same evil; the relegation of life to a lowlier status then a well being' (Daniel Johnson, *The Times*, October 1991). Discuss.

2a Explain how the double effect is used by theologians and philosophers to justify certain forms of euthanasia.

2b Assess the strengths and weaknesses of the double effect argument.

3   Would legislation for voluntary euthanasia destroy the doctor–patient relationship?

4   The case of 'Baby J' (1990). 'Give us that baby. Don't allow it to die. Don't reject it. We will look after him for the rest of his life … It is not for judges to withhold justice on the grounds of quality of life' (Jack Sacrisbrick, the national chairman of LIFE). Assess the arguments of replacing the sanctity of life with the quality of life as the basis for doctor's ethics.

5   Should Christians reject all forms of euthanasia?

6   Discuss how the principle of 'ordinary and extraordinary means' bridges the gap between law and morality in treating the terminally ill. What are the strengths and weaknesses of the principle?

7   Is there a moral difference between cutting short a life and allowing someone to die?

Essay skills

One problem is to define exactly what euthanasia refers to. Define your terms clearly. Some argue that non-voluntary euthanasia is not euthanasia if either the patient is 'dead' or if a patient has not requested it (when it constitutes murder). (Read Chapter 2 on suicide.)

Would legislation for voluntary euthanasia destroy the doctor–patient relationship?
You might consider the logic of the slippery slope or wedge argument and how this might affect legalisation. The wedge argument raises a considerable range of moral and legal issues: autonomy, rights, doctors' duties, killing, resources, quality of life, sanctity of life, protection of the law. Perhaps consider a series of case studies with good grounds for euthanasia and compare these to cases where the only consideration is personal autonomy. Cases A–G are set out in a possible wedge (all are based on or refer to actual cases). In case A quality of life is low and whilst still in sound mind the patient has expressed his wish to die at some future stage. In case G the state is temporary and superficial. Discuss whether legislation would be able to distinguish those who wish to die from those who do not wish to die. Some discussion of autonomy and the paternalism of law should follow. Now consider the patient–doctor relationship. Has your analysis of the cases below suggested that the wedge is a fiction – is this based on real logic or an emotional response? You might wish to conclude with legislation in countries where euthanasia laws have been relaxed (Netherlands).

A. Henry Campbell has had AIDS since 1984 and suffers from pneumonia. His 'living will' signed by his doctor, requests euthanasia when he becomes incapable.

B. Susan has irreversible brain damage. She cannot recognise people or speak meaningfully to them. The family thinks she would want to die and has given permission for the doctors to administer a lethal injection.

C. Tony Bland was severely brain damaged in the Hillsborough football stadium disaster of 1989. He was in a PVS until 1992 when the life-support machine was turned off.

D. James Haig is a man in his twenties paralysed after a car crash. He has managed to set light to his sofa and tried to kill himself. He wants the doctors to assist him to commit suicide.

E. 'Baby J' was severely handicapped (at birth), blind, paralysed and suffered from epilepsy. She was fed through a tube but after a while she was allowed to die at 16 months old.

F. Mary is 14 years old and lives in poverty with her mother. She has just had a baby. She and her mother cannot afford to support the child so have left him to die.

G. A bright sixth-former feels he will let everyone down by doing badly in his exams. He takes an overdose.

5 Killing as Punishment

1 Killing as punishment

> **KEY ISSUE** Dr Johnson once said, 'Depend upon it, Sir, when a man knows he is to be hanged in a fortnight, it concentrates his mind wonderfully' (Boswell, *Life of Johnson*, 19 September 1777).

The issue of capital punishment or state-sanctioned killing as a form of punishment raises many of the same kinds of issues as war and peace (Augustine and Luther both saw war as an extension of capital punishment), only in this case the threat is from individuals within society. However, the context in which capital punishment is considered is sufficiently different to pose quite new considerations. Here the problems are to do with the individual, his or her relationship with the state and the process of law.

> **KEY ISSUE** The issue of judicial killing, the most extreme of all state sanctions, concentrates the mind wonderfully on the reasons for and purpose of punishment in general.

For example, consider the following case of Pat Sonnier's crime and his eventual execution. The case is particularly significant because it involved a Roman Catholic nun, Sister Helen Prejean. The official Roman Catholic view at that time permitted capital punishment only in extreme cases, but experiences like Sister Helen's have convinced them and many Christian Churches that capital punishment is always wrong. The case of Pat Sonnier forms the basis of her book *Dead Man Walking* (1996).

On 7 November, 1977 the *New Iberian* newspaper reported that two young people, both from loving Roman Catholic families, David LeBlanc, 17, and Loretta Bourque, 18, had been shot at close range in the back of the head three times with a .22 rifle. The editorial had concluded: 'It's hard to imagine that there may be somebody in this fine community of ours who could contemplate, much less carry out, this vilest of vile deeds.' On 2 December, 1977 two brothers, Elmo Patrick Sonnier, 27, and Eddie James Sonnier, 20, were accused of having posed as security officers, kidnapped the two teenagers and handcuffed them. They drove the 20 miles and then in the woods Loretta was raped. The brothers ordered both to lie on the ground and then in cold blood shot them. At the trial it was revealed that both men had a long history of offences and came from a poor background. Eddie at first said that Patrick had committed the murders and raped the girl. He had had sex with her because she was willing. Later though, Eddie confessed he had killed the teenagers but his confession was rejected and Patrick was sentenced to death.

The execution takes place:

1   The warden is standing over in the right-hand corner next to a red telephone.

'Have you any last words, Sonnier?' he asks.

'Yes, sir, I do,' Pat says, and he looks at the two fathers, but addresses
5   his words to only one of them. 'Mr LeBlanc, I don't want to leave this world with any hatred in my heart. I want to ask your forgiveness for what me and Eddie done, but Eddie done it.' Mr LeBlanc nods his head. Mr Bourque turns to Mr LeBlanc and asks, 'What about me?'

Pat is in the chair now and guards are moving quickly, removing the leg
10   irons and handcuffs and replacing them with leather straps. One guard had removed his left shoe. They are strapping his trunk, his legs, his arms. He finds my face. He says, 'I love you.' I stretch my hand towards him. 'I love you, too.'

A metal cap is placed on his head and an electrode is screwed in at the
15   top and connected to wire that comes from a box behind the chair. An electrode is fastened to his leg. A strap placed around his chin holds his head tightly against the back of the chair. He grimaces. He cannot speak anymore. A grayish green cloth is placed over his face. I hear three clanks as the switch is pulled with pauses in between. Nineteen hundred
20   volts, then let the body cool, the five hundred volts, pause again, then nineteen hundred volts. 'Christ, be with him, have mercy on him,' I pray simply.

I look up. His left hand has gripped the arm of the chair evenly but the fingers of his right hand are curled upward ... Warden Maggio looks up at the clock and announces the time of death; 12:15 am. His eyes
25   happen to look into mine. He lowers his eyes.

H Prejean, *Dead Man Walking* (1996), pp. 120–1

This case and many others like it from around the world not only raise questions about the use of capital punishment, but the nature and aims of punishment itself.

- Is there are any crime so bad that it permits the state to kill? Does Pat Sonnier deserve to die for his crime?
- Pat came from a very poor, white family. They rarely had enough to eat and so both the men turned to crime from early on in their lives. To what extent should factors like these excuse (or **mitigate**) a crime?
- Has the execution of a man like Pat Sonnier deterred others?
- Is the use of execution a sign that society has failed in its responsibilities to all its citizens?
- Article 5 of the UN Declaration of Human Rights states the 'right not be subjected to torture or to cruel, inhuman or degrading punishment'. Should all civilised societies reject the use of the death penalty?

2 Reasons for and aims of punishment

> **KEY ISSUE** What moral imperatives justify the use of punishment?

In most ordinary moral statements there is usually a relationship between a concrete situation and the reasons derived from it which justify acting in a particular kind of way. A utilitarian might, for instance, argue that stealing is generally wrong because it causes a great deal of anguish and pain. Kantianism argues that lack of respect for property cannot be consistently and universally combined with respect for persons and a stable society. But justifying the moral grounds for punishment is far more elusive.

We can distinguish at this stage between two forms of punishment: **moral punishment** suggests that within any moral system an account is provided for punishment; **legal punishment** suggests that within the judicial process (through statute or common law) the state sanctions various forms of punishment. Clearly the two categories are closely and intimately related to each other. The discussions amongst legal philosophers are complex (see Hart, *The Concept of Law*, 1961, Chapters 8 and 9), but in the case of capital punishment the distinction is particularly significant for it is the *legal* process of killing as punishment which distinguishes it from killing as a private act based on personal moral conscience.

Before we return to the precise moral grounds for punishment, we must first establish what it means to punish. Punishment usually suggests that there is some blame, fault or liability which a person has incurred through act or omission. The punishment awarded is therefore a penalty for a moral or legal failure and by penalty we usually mean a deprivation or suffering of some sort (usually of liberty, property or life). Punishment should be carefully distinguished from *revenge*. For despite their similarities, revenge is the result of personal vendetta whereas punishment is based on moral and/or legal authority. Punishment is considered to be just whereas revenge is not. The conclusion of many philosophers is paradoxical. Although the need for punishment at first appears to be self-evident, the *moral* reasons are often obscure:

> *Why* is the claim that a man has done what he ought not to have done in itself a reason for making him suffer? Why does it give us a permission or whatever? The question has taken several forms, and no satisfactory answer has ever been given.

> T Honderich, *Punishment* (1989), p. 217

1 No ethical theory appears to justify the institution of punishment in its present form. Contending theories of punishment identify flaws in the institution and suggest different and incompatible changes. Meanwhile, since our present practice of punishment appears to serve an essential
5 social purpose in a manner broadly compatible with widely held ethical views, the institution of punishment survives, and shows every sign of doing so for a long time to come.

C Ten, 'Crime and Punishment' in P Singer (ed.), *Companion to Ethics*
(1991), p. 372

The justification for killing as punishment, therefore, must take place within the wider discussion of the aims of punishment.

Traditionally there have been three aims of punishment which have attempted to give moral (and legal) justification for punishment in general and in the particular. This distinction between the general and the particular is important. For whereas we might agree that there are indeed reasons for punishment for infringements of moral or legal rules it is far more complex to decide what *particular* punishment is suitable.

The three aims of punishment are: **retribution**, **reformation** and **deterrence**. Modern thinking on punishment tends towards a consolidated view where none of these aims in themselves is sufficient to provide a comprehensive account. If this is the case, the onus on philosophers is to be able to give accounts which combine these views without compounding the contradictions already inherent in the notion of punishment. One further useful distinction between different aims of punishment is whether the punishment is **backward-looking** or **forward-looking**. In other words, is a punishment isolated *only* with regard to the crime itself or does it consider the long-term, beneficial effects to society as a whole. Considerations of backwards and forward-looking aims of punishment make a considerable difference when deciding on the kinds of punishment implemented in the particular.

a) Retribution

Of all the aims of punishment retribution most clearly expresses what many people instinctively feel is the basis of punishment. It has an ancient history from the law codes of the Babylonian Hammurabi (1728–1686 BCE) to the Old Testament. It is often referred to by Latin *lex talionis* (the Law of the Tooth) 'an eye for an eye, a tooth for a tooth'. In other words, a **grievance** caused requires *satisfaction* on the part of the victim to which he or she (or society) is entitled. Entitlement is for no other reason than that criminals are owed their just **deserts**. Because retribution in its classic formula is backward-looking it should be noted punishment is justified because the criminal deserves it – all other considerations are contingent. So, for instance, the *application* of the punishment is often seen to be important because it reinforces the moral and legal law which has been infringed (i.e. **vindication** or the application of the due process of law).

The problem with retributivism is that it offers no *objective evidence* nor any particular reasoning as to why we should act in this way. Those who utilise retribution have, in the end, to appeal to some form of non-verifiable intuition (we just know) or psychology (another person's suffering cures my own) or mystical (it is in the nature of things) or religious (God demands it) grounds for retribution.

Retributivism has not been in fashion in recent times partly because under the influence of utilitarianism and renewed forms of Christianity it has been regarded as barbaric and void of any human compassion or benevolence. This is particularly evident in the consideration of the offender's motives or intentions.

- To what degree does retributivism take into account the state of mind of the offender by way of mitigation? And if these things are recognised, on what grounds does a retributive theory justify taking age, social status, mental ability, psychology and other factors into account? If this is so, might it then be suggested that these acts were not done with any conscious intent to flout the rules? Of course, the response could be that stealing is stealing, killing is killing, the punishment is the same in each case.
- Most moral and legal systems take account of responsibility or liability. It follows then that to ignore intentions and responsibility for an action for no other reason than actions are actions questions the moral validity of retributive punishment.
- All these criticisms call into question whether retribution can be equitable. At first it seems to treat all like cases the same, but most of us would accept that the moral sensibilities of a child of three are quite different from those of a 14-year-old and must be treated differently. Likewise a person on the brink of death through starvation who steals bread from a shop has a very different motive from someone who steals because it saves them money. Would it be just or fair to punish them in exactly the same way?
- If retribution *does* take some account of mitigation, then it is open to inconsistency where factors which are deemed appropriate in one case are not so in another. These cases do not necessarily rule out retribution, but they pose the complex problem of how a punishment is to be measured.

Yet despite all these objections there is still something essentially satisfying and just about a system of punishment which aims to give back what has been taken by the offender. Honderich outlines some of what has been termed the **new retributivism** (*Punishment*, 1989, pp. 208ff) where some have attempted to see retributivism as a means of paying for rights infringed. The argument here suggests that whereas all other citizens have exercised their *rights* with responsibility and so voluntarily restricted many of their own wishes, it follows that where a person has abused the rights of others by behaving irresponsibly they should lose the very rights they have abused.

Another version attempts to see retribution in terms of a social contract. This, like its rights version, has the advantage of giving an account of where and why punishment is derived. A contract view at least recognises the social context and justification of law and punishment. By contract we mean the self-imposed restrictions which all citizens take on in order to permit other freedoms. It follows that those who have subscribed to the contract which fosters these freedoms has equally agreed to any punishment in advance should they break with the contract.

Finally, there is a more sophisticated version of **restorative retribution** which imposes a burden on the offender as a result of the maldistribution of goods they have caused. In this way their punishment restores the balance of 'goods' they have caused by their offence. Goods has to be interpreted as the *satisfactions* associated with goods and not the goods themselves (this would pose insuperable practical problems). All these views (and there are several others) are attempts to remove the obscurity on which traditional retributivism is based and suggest a more objective basis for punishment. In addition they at least try to take into account the problem of equity and responsibility to satisfy specific grievances (see Honderich, *Punishment*, 1989, for a more detailed analysis).

b) Deterrence

At the other end of retributive punishment is deterrence. Deterrence has a forward-looking view of punishment because it views punishment essentially as a means of enabling society to function fully in the future. This view is not ruled out by the retributivist (and especially with the new retributive arguments) as an aim of punishment, but the difference is that the deterrent view does not punish the offence for its own sake. The deterrent argument is classically the lynchpin of utilitarianism and especially its founding father Jeremy **Bentham** (1748–1832). In his *Principles of Penal Law* Bentham argued that:

- punishment is unnecessary if the offence will not recur;
- punishment is only appropriate to dissuade others from behaving in the same way;
- punishment is, therefore, to protect society for the future.

The utilitarian principle is bound to regard punishment itself as undesirable. According to the utilitarian maxim (or aim) of maximising happiness and avoiding pain, any deliberate infliction of pain could only be justified utilitarianly provided it resulted in greater happiness or satisfactions. The strength of this view is that it is able to look at each case with some degree of independence. It exercises a *minimising policy,* i.e. that punishment should inflict the least amount of pain possible. Its form of punishment and justice is always *distributive* and for the benefit of all, not a minority. And finally it allows the offender the opportunity to reform and seeks to prevent crime rather than wait for harm to be done.

Criticisms of the deterrent position fall into two kinds: observational and philosophical. The substantial claim of the utilitarian position is that it can offer objective evidence for the implementation of punishment. It is an argument so widely employed that its truth is hardly questioned. And yet in all empirical study it is far from certain whether punishment does necessarily deter others from wrong-doing. Of course it *may* do so, but with what certainty and with what degree of reliability? Does it make the good citizen better and wash over the habitual offender? Statistics without considerable justification can be manipulated to suit diametrically opposed causes. If deterrence fails on the objective level what are the philosophical problems?

The most often cited objection is that it is open to *unfairness* and despite its humanitarian concern for the individual it could justify some forms of punishment which retributivists would find abhorrent. Some objectors cite a story along the lines first put forward by E F Carritt (*Ethical and Political Thinking,* 1947): a judge decides to hang an innocent man because it is widely believed that he is guilty of murders and his death will act as a necessary deterrence for the death of innocent people in the future. MacIntyre for instance concludes:

1 For by allowing the principle of utility to override our existing principles – such that a man ought not to be hanged for a crime which he has not committed – we remove one more barrier to using the concept of the general happiness to license any enormity. That it can be
5 so used has been amply demonstrated in this century; in particular the high-minded are apt to use totalitarianism as a justification to excuse their responsibility for involvement in such large-scale crimes of their societies, such as Auschwitz or Hiroshima.

A. MacIntyre, *A Short History of Ethics*, p. 240

Honderich accuses utilitarianism of **victimisation** (*Punishment*, 1989, p. 62). The responses to this are very varied. Some Utilitarians follow Mill (**weak rule utilitarianism**) and argue that if there is general disapproval of punishing the innocent then the introduction of a rule forbidding this kind of deterrent punishment would avoid the possibility of the 'punishment' of the innocent. Even so, there exists the possibility that in classical act utilitarianism the justification might be as Caiaphas is reported to have said, 'it is expedient for you that one man should die for the people' (John 11:50).

Finally there is Kant's criticism of utilitarianism in general and punishment in particular. According to the first formulation of the categorical imperative it is impossible to allow an innocent man to suffer, but the second or 'practical imperative' states that people should never be used as a means to an end – and this would rule out *all* forms of punishment as deterrent. For in every case offenders would be treated as a means to an end and not as an end in themselves. Such a view ignores them as human beings and divests them of any intrinsic value or at the very least plays down their own interests (which is especially important for the reformative view of punishment). Of course, Bentham and the utilitarian tradition acknowledge that punishment does entail some loss of dignity on the part of the punished offender; if it did not there would be no deterrent effect on others. However, the utilitarian principle still does not give an objective means for estimating the proportion of punishment, other than the minimum necessary to deter others.

c) Reform

Reformative punishment is forward-looking and shares many of the characteristics of deterrence. Where it differs is in its consideration of the status of the offender. It sees punishment as both the means and opportunity to return the offender back into society as a useful member. It shares some of the retributivist's desires to allow an offender to feel that they have paid off or atoned for their guilt, but goes further in seeing this as a positive process for the future. Some aims of reform are less extravagant and hope at least to make the offender more law abiding (even if this is just a fear of being caught and punished again). Other reform aims might include a more compassionate or benevolent understanding of the motives or factors which led to the offence. The reformer looks in particular at the mental and physical state of the offender. These factors not only mitigate the crime but also suggest that society is obliged to help the offender overcome his or her difficulties. Our knowledge of psychology has helped us to sympathise with the offender who has not acted entirely through his or her own conscious will but is affected by repressed experiences from his past (or other psychological imbalances).

But why should the aim of punishment be to instil certain moral values? Why should these values necessarily be the right ones and is prison the best way to impart them? Not all offenders feel that they have done anything morally wrong and any attempt to reform their views may simply reinforce their beliefs. Within liberal thinking it may be appropriate to learn respect for the law, but basic liberties entitle a person to hold their own views and values.

● Reform could be construed as an unnecessary infringement of personal autonomy.

- The issues raised by **psychology** are open to considerable discussion; there are Orwellian worries that if prison is seen to be the place to have these imbalances 'corrected' then any misdemeanour might give the state the excuse needed to turn out 'balanced' citizens (through indoctrination).
- Perhaps this is another form of victimisation to which Honderich objects (*Punishment*, 1989, p. 102).
- Others, like C S Lewis (*The Humanitarian Theory of Punishment*, 1953), accuse such 'humanitarian' forms of punishment of diminishing the offender's sense of just desert and in doing so reducing his or her dignity.

3 Capital punishment

So we now turn specifically to the ultimate punitive sanction considered against the various criticisms associated with retribution, deterrence and reformation. Already, in the aims of punishment outlined above it has been necessary to give one example of capital punishment as an extreme illustration associated with punishment.

a) Historical background

The history of capital punishment over the past two hundred years is of particular interest and importance because it illustrates how each of the aims of punishment has been tried and tested in public debate, concluding in 1965 in the UK with the abolition of capital punishment.

'THE BLOODY CODE'

England in the eighteenth century had more provisions for the **Bloody Code** (as it was frequently referred to) than any other European country:

1723   Waltham Black Act set out 50 possible offences including forgery of birth, baptism, marriage certificates; arson; attempted murder of parents; picking a pocket of more than one shilling. A great number of punishments were over property offences.
1837   Reform had reduced the number of offences to sixteen.
1841   Hanging for rape was abolished reducing the charges to seven.
1868   The last public hanging was held.
1922   The Infanticide Act abolished hanging for mothers who killed their new-born children.
1931   Sentence of Death (Expectant Mothers) Act abolished hanging for pregnant women.
1933   The Children and Young Persons Act abolished hanging for those under 18. In the years leading up to abolition the debate was whether capital punishment should be reserved only for first degree murder, i.e. premeditated murder.

The modern debate begins with an essay by **Beccaria**, *On Crimes and Punishment* (1764) with an abolitionist argument that was to be employed time and time again until the repeal of capital acts. Beccaria argued that deterrence was the only morally sound basis for capital punishment, but it did not deter and an enlightened society should therefore work for prevention of crime not punishment. In particular Beccaria argued that capital punishment was inconsistently and indiscriminately employed.

The hanging of Derek Bentley in 1953 sparked off widespread abolitionist feeling amongst the general public. Bentley had been an accomplice to a burglary which had resulted in the shooting of a police officer. At the time of the shooting he had been in police custody, but Christopher Craig, who had actually shot the round, was too young to be charged with the capital offence. An increasing sense of injustice coupled with a tide of popular moral repulsion swelled sufficiently to bring Parliament to the stage where the abolition of the death penalty was considered to be the only logical step to reform the law. Bentley's pardon was finally granted posthumously in August 1998. But a determining factor was the Church which for so long had supported the *status quo* and which now, after an eloquent speech by the Archbishop of Canterbury, tipped the balance in favour of abolition (see Potter, *Hanging in Judgement*, 1993, ch. 17). Finally in 1965 the Murder (Abolition of Death Penalty) Act was passed for a trial period and affirmed on the 16 and 18 December, 1969. Under the influence of the European Convention on Human Rights, The Crime and Disorder Act (1998) removed treason and piracy (the two remaining grounds for capital punishment) from the statute books.

At the present time the debate is most fiercely contended in the USA where the death penalty was reintroduced in certain states from 1977 onwards. The present useage of capital punishment worldwide can be seen in Table 4.

b) Retributive arguments for capital punishment

Each of the following arguments must be read in the wider context of punishment outlined above.

The retributive arguments have a long and ancient history particularly in the West because of the support of biblical and Church traditions. Throughout the modern debates and particularly in the eighteenth and nineteenth centuries the retributive debates have frequently made use of such texts as:

> Genesis 9:6 "Whoever sheds the blood of man, by man shall his blood be shed; for God made man in his own image." (see also Leviticus 24:17)

> Romans 13:4 "But if you do wrong, be afraid, for he does not bear the sword in vain; he is the servant of God to execute his wrath on the wrongdoer".

Table 4 The present state of capital punishment worldwide

Amnesty International reports that:
- 67 countries and territories have abolished the death penalty for all crimes; 14 countries have abolished the death penalty for all but exceptional crimes such as wartime crimes; 23 countries can be considered abolitionist de facto: they retain the death penalty in law but have not carried out any executions for the past 10 years or more making a total of 104 countries which have abolished the death penalty in law or practice.

  (List of Abolitionist and Retentionist Countries, *AI Index*: ACT 50/08/98)
- 91 other countries retain and use the death penalty, but the number of countries which actually execute prisoners in any one year is much smaller.
- During 1997, 2,607 prisoners are known to have been executed in 40 countries and 4,364 sentenced to death in 69 countries. These are the figures reported to AI – the true figures are certainly higher.

  (Death Sentences and Executions in 1997, *AI Index*: ACT 51/01/98)

United States of America
- 45 prisoners were executed in the USA in 1996 and 11 from January 1997 to 25 March 1997, bringing to 366 the total number executed since the use of the death penalty was resumed in 1977.
- Over 3,150 prisoners were under sentence of death at the end of September 1996. 38 of the 50 US states now provide for the death penalty in law; the death penalty is also provided under US Federal military and civilian law.

  (United States of America: Developments on the Death Penalty in 1996, *AI Index*: AMR 51/01/97)

Treaties
- The Sixth Protocol to the European Convention on Human Rights Concerning the Abolition of the Death Penalty (1950): ratified by 30 European countries and signed by three others (see *When the State Kills*, p. 249 for extracts).
- The Protocol to the American Convention on Human Rights to Abolish the Death Penalty: ratified by six US states and signed by one other.

In other words the Bible provided the objective evidence to justify the *lex talionis* which lies at the heart of retribution. Punishment is awarded on the grounds that because an offence has been committed the just desert, religiously, morally and legally, is to act on behalf of God who demands satisfaction with the death of a sinner. There are many objections to the use of these biblical texts within a wider theological debate which will be discussed below. As an alternative to the biblical 'objectivity' Kant's philosophical argument (*Philosophy of Law*) was an attempt to provide a non-metaphysical but transcendental (or universal) justification for the traditional retributive argument. Note that his argument begins with the moral reasons for capital punishment which provide the basis for legal capital punishment.

1   If Justice and Righteousness perish, human life would no longer have any value in the world. – What, then, is to be said of such a proposal as to keep a Criminal alive who has been condemned to death, on his being given to understand that if he agreed to certain dangerous experiments being
5   performed on him, he would be allowed to survive if he came happily through them? ... a Court of Justice would repudiate with scorn any proposal of this kind if made to it by the Medical Faculty; for Justice would cease to be Justice if it were bartered away for any consideration whatever.
Even if a Civil Society resolved to dissolve itself with the consent of
10   all its members – as might be supposed in the case of a People inhabiting an island resolving to separate and scatter themselves through the whole world – the last Murderer lying in the prison ought to be executed before the resolution was carried out. This ought to be done in order that every one may realise the desert of his deeds, and
15   the blood-guiltiness may not remain upon the people; for otherwise they might all be regarded as participators in the murder as a public violation of justice.

from *Philosophy of Law,* quoted in T Honderich, *Punishment*
(1989), p. 22

The main points of Kant's argument are:

● Retribution precedes any good to the offender. By this Kant rules out any reformative or deterrent aims of punishment *in the first instance*. An offender is punished because he 'has committed a crime' and deserves it.
● Justice and righteousness are the bedrock on which human value or dignity depends. Because Kant's view of morality is universal ('Act as if the maxim of your action were to become through your will a universal law') and murder is always the most heinous infringement of human liberty, then it follows that in permitting a murderer to live one is undermining the essential values on which society is founded.
● A murderer ought to be executed in order to see that just deserts have been awarded. No other punishment is suitable; killing cannot be 'bartered' with a lesser punishment.
● Failure to punish condemns a society, otherwise it might be construed that in failing to punish it is condoning murder. A judge is **categorically obliged** (there is no distinction between moral and legal obligation) to apply the law and ignore mitigating circumstances.
● 'Blood-guiltiness may not remain on the people.' Kant seems here to appeal to the mystical notion that blood for blood satisfies a very deep

human psychological need. There is certainly a long tradition to which the Bible witnesses (e.g. after Abel's murder by Cain 'the voice of your brother's blood is crying to me from the ground' Genesis 4:10) that the death of an offender in some way atones for the death of their victim. There is circumstantial evidence, often cited by **retentionists**, that even the offender realises this and *wants* to die. There is a great deal made of this in the mid-nineteenth century when the priest's job with the condemned was to evince a confession of guilt (see Potter, *Hanging in Judgement*, 1993, ch. 9), not just because it offered the possibility of salvation but because by acknowledging the guilt of their crime the criminal removed the stain of the offence from society.

The **abolutionist** arguments against retribution use many of the criticisms of retribution above. The history of the move away from capital punishment shows an increasing awareness that motives must be taken seriously. Account is taken of age, psychological state and provocation. Ironically the 'confession' so much sought by the nineteenth-century prison chaplains and the experience of prison visitors and lawyers today often confirm that the offender is not a 'bad person'. This experience is particularly the criticism of the reformist. In an attempt to offer a less harsh version of Kant's rejection of mitigation ('barter' as he calls it), the historical development of capital punishment has increasingly led to great inconsistency. The retributive aim founders most here where a lack of objective assessment makes it impossible to determine the level of responsibility which establishes a person's guilt. The Bentley case has come to illustrate the importance which many people place on degrees of responsibility and guilt. This is not to say that reduced responsibility mitigates *all* retributive punishment. So is there a case to be made for capital punishment based on **new retributivism**?

The **rights retributive** argument was first put forward by Thomas **Aquinas**, although not stated as a 'rights' argument as we would understand it today. Aquinas first argues for the **deterrent effect** of capital punishment but goes on to argue:

1   In doing wrong men depart from the order laid down by reason, falling away from their human dignity in which they are by nature free and exist for their own sake into the subject state of animals that must serve the needs of others. So it becomes justifiable to kill a malefactor
5   as one would kill an animal. 'An evil man,' says Aristotle, 'is worse than an animal and more harmful.' But the care of the whole community is entrusted to those exercising public authority, and so only they, not private persons, may licitly execute malefactors. We cannot distinguish malefactors from just men by nature; they can only be differentiated by
10 a public judgement.

Summa Theologiae, IIae 2:64

Aquinas maintains, as do many people today, that there are some crimes which are so heinous and of such magnitude that however one regards the mitigating circumstances, a person has demeaned themselves to such an extent that they have abrogated any rights which might be due to them. Aquinas justifies death as part of the natural order of things; just as (by analogy) we are entitled to kill animals for food and protection, so therefore we may also take a criminal's life whose actions show them to be no more than an animal. In this way the traditional backward-looking 'guilt–desert' formula is preserved, but the justification is sufficiently forward-looking and situational to regard each case separately.

However, Aquinas' argument would probably fail to find much support from rights movements today. Firstly it is dubious whether the *International Bill of Human Rights* would permit capital punishment, on the grounds that capital punishment disregards 'the right to life' (Article 3). Secondly, under Article 5, 'the right not to be subjected to torture or to cruel, inhuman or degrading punishment', capital punishment is almost always regarded as a barbaric and unacceptable means by which a modern state should operate.

The contract view is attractive because of its simplicity. Citizens accept that in return for the protection which the state gives them they are liable for any punishments which have been agreed upon for the well-running of society if they should break their side of the contract. This may include capital punishment. Again this touches on the deterrent argument but is essentially backward-looking, because, it is argued, a citizen knows what the law is and if he or she chooses to break it, then he or she can expect to receive his or her just deserts. However, it is still possible to employ mitigation arguments. Furthermore, as Honderich argues, it is questionable to what degree any citizen is really under contract as it is the legislators and not the citizens who are the designers of the contract and its laws. Past legislation (e.g. the Waltham Black Act of 1723) has suggested that in practice capital punishment can be introduced for comparatively trivial offences to which it is hard to envisage any ordinary person subscribing. In the end contract retributivism does not seem to achieve the degree of objectivity sufficient to justify taking a man's life.

Restorative retribution is a less obscure version of Kant's blood-guiltiness. However, it suffers from a lack of objective or empirical basis. It might be possible literally to allow the victims of murder to settle on some punishment which they feel would adequately recompense them (such as money or death as Islamic law permits in some countries). But it is very hard to know whether capital punishment would really have the desired effect in seeking fairly to distribute recompense for grievances experienced throughout society.

c) Deterrent arguments for capital punishment

Many of the new retributive arguments for capital punishment have more than hinted at the beneficial side-effects for society and possibly even the offender (through repentance). The deterrent argument is therefore a forward-looking alternative, though not necessarily incompatible with the retributivist viewpoint. The emotional argument for deterrence is as powerful an intuition as that of retribution. Take for instance the statement of the famous Victorian lawyer Sir James Fitzjames Stephen in 1864:

1 No other punishment deters men so effectually from committing crimes as the punishment of death. This is one of those propositions which is difficult to prove, simply because they are in themselves more obvious than any proof can make them. It is possible to display
5 ingenuity in arguing against it, but that is all. The whole experience of mankind is in the other direction.

'Capital Punishments' in *Fraser's Magazine*

It might be argued that in order to be effective capital punishment should be as public as possible. During the nineteenth century the process and *ritual* of hanging was so refined that it took on the guise of a dramatic morality play. Through it the crowds could watch as the prisoner, led by the chaplain to the gallows, delivered a moralising 'sermon' (often taught by the chaplain) warning them not to copy his or her example of crime, followed by his or her death. At its crudest and most immediate this is the deterrent argument (see Potter, *Hanging in Judgement*, ch. 6). However, as history has demonstrated, the spectacle of a hanging could equally have the effect of turning people *against* the death penalty and making them regard the law as barbaric and unjust. For instance in July 1840 the two celebrated writers William Makepeace Thackeray and Charles Dickens witnessed the hanging of Francois Courvoisier. Both men were so appalled at the brutality of what they had seen that they turned their literary skills to the abolitionist cause (see Dickens, *Barnaby Rudge*, ch. 78). There was also considerable concern that hanging had become an excuse for bad behaviour and salacious spectacle. In 1868 hanging became a private affair conducted within the prison. The last vestige of religious meaning was abolished in 1927 when chaplains were forbidden to read the burial service.

Retentionists play heavily on the good effects that the death penalty has protecting society from further harm and discouraging others from carrying out killings. For example, one retentionist quotes the research shown in Table 5.

Table 5 Executions and murders in USA 1960–76		
Date	Executions	Number of murders
1960	56	9,140
1964	15	9,250
1969	none	14,590
1972–6	capital punishment suspended	20,510 (1975)
1976	reintroduction of the death penalty	12% drop

Source: Texas A&M University.

On the other hand abolitionists such as Amnesty International quote the situation in Canada where, 17 years after abolition, the murder rate is 27 per cent lower than in 1976. AI quotes (see *When the State Kills*, 1989, pp. 10–14) the conclusions of a report made by the United Nations in 1988:

1 This research has failed to provide scientific proof that executions have a greater deterrent effect than life imprisonment. Such proof is unlikely to be forthcoming. The evidence as a whole still gives no positive support to the deterrent hypothesis.

5 The fact that all the evidence continues to point in the same direction is persuasive *a priori* evidence that countries need not fear sudden and serious changes in the curve of crime if they reduce their reliance on the death penalty.

Given the ambiguity of the statistics some argue for a best bet position. If, therefore, the evidence is unclear whether capital punishment does or does not deter we are left either way gambling with people's lives. It is therefore worthwhile using the death penalty as deterrence to save *innocent* people's lives rather than preserving the lives of those who are guilty and maybe in doing so failing to deter murderers from taking innocent lives.

A utilitarian who advocates the death penalty has to justify why death is appropriate when prison without parole may have equivalent deterrent effect *and* also minimalise suffering caused to the offender (see Bentham's aims above). J S Mill for instance, in his famous address to Parliament in 1868, argued that capital punishment expresses the public's trust in the legal system and for law and order:

1 to deter by suffering from inflicting suffering is not only possible, but the very purpose of penal justice. Does fining a criminal show want of respect for property, or imprisoning him, for personal freedom? Just as unreasonable is it to think that to take a life of a man who has taken

5 that of another is to show want of regard for human life. We show, on the contrary, most emphatically our regard for it, by the adoption of a rule that he who violates that right of another forfeits it for himself,

and that while no other crime that he can commit deprives him of his right to live, this shall.

from 'Parliamentary Debate on Capital Punishment Within Prisons Bill (1868)', reprinted in P Singer, *Applied Ethics* (1986)

Those who favour the death penalty argue that the finality of capital punishment secures peace of mind. They argue that there is a chance that the prisoner might escape, or the prison system might be altered with new legislation or a more sympathetic view of parole might permit a prisoner to be released later. But in practice there are very few cases where prisoners have escaped and reoffended and the Utilitarian could be just as secure in mind that the prisoner has been locked away for ever without having to add unnecessary pain through execution.

Supposing the evidence for deterrence could be demonstrated unequivocally to work, would this inevitably lead one to advocate capital punishment? Do I become culpable if I refrain from carrying out executions (i.e. my failure to act has resulted in the death/ murders of innocent people) because I believe that killing is wrong? One line of defence might be to call on the **acts and omissions** doctrine. I might reasonably argue that I cannot be blamed for something which I have not done. So, for instance, I cannot be blamed for failing to help those who have died from starvation after drought in a distant country when I am not in a position to do so. Or in another situation if, as a pacifist, I refrain from fighting a war can I be blamed for the deaths of my compatriots?

So, if in the case of capital punishment I hold that killing people is wrong then it follows that I must not directly cause the death of a murderer and in refraining from doing so I cannot be directly blamed for any subsequent murder victims because of my omission. But the acts and omissions argument does not convince most consequentialists, traditional utilitarians and Natural Law moralists (see page 61 on euthanasia). An omission which results in a lesser good, they argue, must be treated as a blameworthy act. If one rejects the acts and omissions doctrine, as Jonathan Glover does (see *Causing Death and Saving Lives*, 1977, p. 94), then the case for capital punishment on the conclusive evidence that it does deter further deaths, becomes inevitable.

The other criticisms are outlined above in the general consideration of deterrence and centre on the justification for the execution of an innocent man for the good of society. The argument depends on the existence of other moral sensitivities which can be considered really as the side-effects of capital punishment. Utilitarians might want to consider the painful effects on the executed man's friends, family and other prisoners. Then there might simply be the brutalising effect executions might have on society as a whole, and knowledge of the actual process of an execution may generally cause many people great unease about the society they live in.

d) Reform arguments for capital punishment

The only arguments which can be made for capital punishment as reform fall under the deterrent argument. As we have seen, the retributivist has also regarded the reform of the offender as an important part of the process of atoning for blood-guiltiness and as an example to others. However, the reformist position has been one which looks less at the victims of crime and more at the humanity of the offender. The reformist position inevitably leads to a broadly anti-death-penalty position.

Some of the leading abolitionists in nineteenth-century England were Quakers. Their arguments rested on a number of important Christian precepts which had been obscured in favour of the retributive argument. These are broadly based on the sanctity of life argument but include the Christian moral imperative to save the sinner so that they may return to society. The Anglican Prayer Book (1662) prayer for the absolution of sins (after the prayer of confession) states:

1 Almighty God, the Father of our Lord Jesus Christ, who desireth not the death of a sinner, but rather that he may turn from his wickedness and live; and hath given power and commandment to his Ministers, to declare and pronounce to his people, being penitent, the Absolution
5 and Remission of their sins.

Jesus' treatment of the woman caught in adultery (John 8:3–11) where Jesus commutes her death penalty and, in general, all the New Testament texts (see below) which presented Christianity as a religion of compassion, forgiveness and rehabilitation, contributed to a decisive swing away from the Mosaic law of vengeance depicted in the Hebrew Bible (Old Testament). In Matthew 5:38–39 Jesus specifically replaces the *lex talionis* with an ethic of reconciliation:

You have heard that it was said 'An eye for an eye and a tooth for a tooth'. But I say to you, Do not resist one who is evil. But if anyone strikes you on the right cheek, turn to him the other also.

For many reformists capital punishment rests on a moral contradiction that permits the killing of a person (even though they may be guilty) because they have killed. The anomaly is considered even less satisfactory when the authority of the state to kill places itself above personal moral behaviour.

4 Theological considerations

KEY ISSUE The Christian Church has over the centuries held diametrically opposed views regarding the death penalty.

In the UK over the past two hundred years the abolitionist cause was both hindered and eventually won by the views of the Church. In the USA today, where capital punishment is practised and much debated, the retentionist cause is part of the credo of many conservative Christians.

a) The Bible

The issue here is the relationship between the Old and New Testaments. Those who advocate the death penalty refer to Genesis 9:6, 'Whoever sheds the blood of man, by man shall his blood be shed; for God made man in his own image' (see also Leviticus 24:17) and Romans 13:4, 'But if you do wrong, be afraid, for he does not bear the sword in vain; he is the servant of God to execute his wrath on the wrongdoer'. Often referred to are Jesus' words to the penitent robber (Luke 23:39–43) who died on the cross next to Him. As some commentators argue, Jesus does not absolve the man of his crime nor condemn the nature of his punishment but He does promise him eternal bliss as a reward for his repentance. The retentionist argument also refers to events where God killed as the punishment for sins. Genesis 6 recounts the destruction of mankind through a flood; the inhabitants of Sodom were destroyed because of gross acts of inhospitality (possibly rape) and Ananias and Sapphira were struck down because they failed to disclose to the Apostles all the money they had made on the sale of some property (Acts 5:1–11). There are any number of cases in the Old Testament which required the death penalty: adultery (Deuteronomy 22:22), dishonour to parents (Exodus 21:15), a stranger who enters the Temple (Numbers 1:51) and magic (Leviticus 20:27).

There are many responses to reading the Bible in this way. The contribution of scholars such as the nineteenth-century Old Testament scholar Julius Wellhausen have argued that there is an evolutionary revelation from Old to New Testament. Thus the punishments of the Old Testament are for a very different society from the one in which Jesus delivered his revelation. 'You have heard it said' is replaced or modified with 'but I say to you'. Others point to the pattern of Jesus' own life as the template for Christian behaviour and avoid quoting texts out of context of His whole message. Working within the general 'spirit' of Christ is not retributive but compassionate, forgiving and loving. This is the line which the Archbishop of Canterbury, William Temple, took in a hugely influential paper reprinted in 1934 by *The Spectator*.

1 The present discussion of the Death Penalty has an importance that
extends far beyond the subject itself. The retention or alteration of our
present practice, now that the question has been sharply raised, must
depend upon the moral principles accepted by the community for the
5 government of its penal code. Recent experience has shown that in
many cases public opinion revolts against the execution of condemned
criminals and indeed the proportion of reprieves tends steadily to
increase. Moreover, observation seems to leave no doubt with regard
to the chief quality of effectiveness in deterrent punishment. It is not
10 the severity of the penalty inflicted, but the certainty both of detection
and of the exaction of the penalty required by law, whatever this may
be. If then, as seems unquestionable, we have reached a stage where the
expectation of execution has been rendered definitely uncertain, so
that there is always a hope of reprieve, the death penalty will be less of
15 a deterrent than a life sentence without possibility of reprieve. What is
required for effective deterrence is that there shall be prescribed for
the crime a penalty which will then and there be inflicted. Our modern
sentiment has robbed the death penalty of its chief defence. Unless,
therefore, it can be pleaded that the penalty is uniquely deterrent,
20 which in modern conditions it is not, the case against it seems
overwhelming.

    There is one other consideration which we have kept to the end
because it is of quite supreme importance. It is the principle laid down
by Jeremy Bentham that the State affects the conduct and actions of its
25 citizens more by the standards governing its own action than by the
penalties which it visits upon others. It is often said that execution for
murder is justified because murder, being an outrage upon the sanctity
of life, calls for a quite unique retribution or repudiation. That in itself may
be true: but the State will do most to promote regard for the sanctity of
30 life by paying regard to that sanctity itself. Its action in taking life where
murder is proved will do more to undermine regard for life, and
therefore even to encourage murder, than the terrible nature of the
punishment could do to check murderous impulse. This is an argument
which in any special application is incapable of being tested; but the
35 principle of it rests both upon a very wide observation of instances and
upon the understanding of human character possessed by those who
have most deeply penetrated its secrets.

from 'The Death Penalty' in The Spectator, 25 January, 1935
(written when Temple was Archbishop of York)

b) Authority and judgement

A more thorny theological issue is to what degree do humans, the
Church or the state have God's authority to carry out His judgement.
In Matthew 16:18–19 Peter is told:

> And I tell you, you are Peter, and on this rock I will build my church, and the powers of death will not prevail against it. I will give you the keys of the kingdom of heaven, and whatever you bind on earth will be bound in heaven, and what ever you loose on earth will be loosed in heaven.

The power invested in Peter to bind and loose is taken to mean the forgiveness and condemnation of sins. But there is no consensus as to what *degree* is permitted to the Christian community. There are three possibilities. **Maximum authority**: the community acts as God's agents on earth, and taking the lead from Genesis 9 this authorises man to carry out punishment (and capital punishment). If God's Kingdom is to be established on earth then in the face of evil extreme action has sometimes to be exercised. **Minimum authority**: the community acts only insofar as it prepares the individual for the coming of God's final judgement. Jesus' death on the cross takes on human guilt so that retributive justice is now redundant. **Restrained authority**: the previous model perhaps dwelt too much on final judgement leaving too little to be exercised in the present. In Romans 13 Paul depicts a long-term view of society which requires institutions, laws and punishments (the 'sword' should not be taken literally but as a symbol of authority). The Christian community is given authority to judge but not so that it creates terror (the danger with a maximum model), but with mercy and restraint. In the story of Cain, Cain was pardoned by God although he deserved to die for having killed Abel (Genesis 4:15). The natural desire to seek vengeance is transmuted into a life where Cain atones for his own sin.

c) Salvation

The use of punishment therefore not only serves to prepare the individual for God's judgement but also to establish through **social control** God's Kingdom or rule on earth (see the injunction in the Lord's Prayer – 'thy will be done on earth as it is in heaven'). The question *today* for churches working in secular societies is whether there can be legitimate use of capital punishment given that there are many effective alternatives.

The Roman Catholic Church's view is expressed in the encyclical *Evangelium Vitae* (The Gospel of Life) issued 25 March, 1995. John Paul II wrote that execution is only appropriate 'in cases of absolute necessity, in other words, when it would not be possible otherwise to defend society. Today, however, as a result of steady improvement in the organisation of the penal system, such cases are very rare, if not practically non-existent'. The position is one set out also in the *Catechism of the Catholic Church* (1994, p. 488).

1 Preserving the common good of society requires rendering the aggressor unable to inflict harm. For this reason the traditional teaching of the Church has acknowledged as well-founded the right and duty of legitimate public authority to punish malefactors by means of penalties

5   commensurate with the gravity of the crime, not excluding, in cases of extreme gravity, the death penalty. For analogous reasons those holding authority have the right to repel by armed force aggressors against the community in their charge.

Both statements are very wary about the use of the death penalty and shy away from a retributive argument in favour of protection/ deterrence. Where possible, punishment should be reformative both for the good of the offender and for society (as atonement).

It is not surprising, therefore, that the recent *Corrigenda* (1999) of the *Catechism* has included the quotation from *Evangelium Vitae* and reinforced the view that non-lethal methods of punishment should be preferred to protect people's safety. In other words, the present Roman Catholic view allows for the wicked to be punished but limits capital punishment to very rare occasions. Total exclusion of capital punishment would weaken the Church's view of war and the possibility of killing the wicked in that context.

Answering structured and essay questions

Summary

1   *Killing as punishment.*

2   *Reasons and aims of punishment:* moral punishment and legal punishment. Forward- and backward-looking nature of punishment.

    a)   Retribution: satisfaction, vindication, motives, equity, new retributivism, restorative retributivism.

    b)   Deterrence: Bentham, unfairness, victimisation, Kant's criticism.

    c)   Reform: compassion, infringement of autonomy.

3   *Capital punishment:*

    a)   Historical background: Beccaria, Bloody Code, Murder (Abolition of Death Penalty) Act, Crime and Disorder Act. Practices worldwide.

    b)   Retributive arguments for capital punishment: Kant (just deserts, blood-guiltiness), Aquinas. Contract and protection. Restorative retribution.

    c)   Deterrent arguments for capital punishment: public effect, best bet argument, acts and omissions.

    d)   Reform arguments for capital punishment: repentance inconsistency of treating like with like.

    e)   Theological arguments: The Bible. William Temple (quote some suitable passages for your essays). Authority of the Church. Types of authority. Salvation. Roman Catholic Church views.

Questions

1a Explain why some people argue that the main purpose of punishment is retributive.

1b Discuss the moral reasons why capital punishment is not a just or fair form of punishment.

2a Compare and contrast the arguments of Kant, Mill and Temple for and against capital punishment.

2b Discuss who offers the most persuasive argument.

3 'In a society where there is a good prison system Christian theology cannot justify the death penalty.' Discuss.

4 A person knows that if he murders then he will hang for it. Is it reasonable for him to be killed by the state if he is then found guilty of homicide?

5 If capital punishment could be shown to be an effective deterrence on future potential murderers, should it then be reintroduced into the UK?

6 Does a retributive form of punishment rule out deterrence and reform as equally important aims of punishment? Discuss with particular reference to capital punishment.

Essay skills

In most essays on capital punishment two things have to be borne in mind. First, all discussion of capital punishment has to be within the context of the aims and purposes of punishment in general. Secondly, the moral reasons for punishment are frequently more difficult to justify than appears at first. Use the historical section of this chapter to provide examples from the past, or use present examples from around the world.

If capital punishment could be shown to be an effective deterrence on future potential murderers, should it then be reintroduced into the UK?

This essay proposes the most persuasive view of capital punishment but it will require some reference to the other aims of punishment. Consider the utilitarian viewpoint. The utilitarian argument has to justify inflicting pain for the greatest happiness – look at Glover's conclusion. The weakness of the view is that the same deterrent effect could be achieved by executing an innocent person. Many would regard this as grossly immoral. Consider the best bet response to this.

You should then ask whether the law should be changed. A *brief* outline of the historical reasons why it was abolished might suggest why society has changed its views. You might look at the reform view of punishment and the inconsistency of treating killing with killing. You could suggest that alternatives such as life imprisonment could equally satisfy the aims of reform and deterrence.

Finally you might wish to consider whether deterrence is more effective if it includes the backward aims retributive justice/ punishment. By way of conclusion you could refer to the recent change in Roman Catholic traditional teaching and consider whether capital punishment causes more moral outrage than effective deterrence.

6 War and Peace

1 War and social order

KEY ISSUE The issue of war is frequently less to do with the morality of killing than the legitimacy of maintaining or establishing social order.

Even those who most vehemently oppose all forms of violence do so because they have a vision of a society where non-violence in its widest sense is the key factor which governs all human relationships. In that sense war is not a moral issue; it is simply not an option. At the other end of the scale there are those who argue that war is the driving force of the state, it is the means by which the values of the state are expressed, such as strength, honour, loyalty and so on. Again there is no moral *issue* here: war is not a means to be debated but an end in itself. These two lines of thought, the **pacifist** and **militarist**, cut across all political ideologies, although in practice pacifism is closer to the democracies of the West and militarism is often equated with fascism and certain forms of political/religious fundamentalism. There is much in common between these two positions in their **utopian** view of the state (i.e. an ideal state which will be established in the future). Both believe that the use or non-use of war are **expressive** of higher beliefs.

To these we must add two other related arguments. The **realist** and **just war argument** (JWA) both recognise that war is sometimes a necessary **instrument** of state. These two instrumental views of war are enormously important in what they tell us about the relationship of public and private morality. The realist argues that where the state is concerned the complexities of private morality cannot and should not be transferred wholesale into the public arena. So for instance, I might as a private citizen choose never to punish my children but allow them to find out their morality by trial and error. But this would never work on a large scale without chaos and possible violence. Public morality has largely to disregard the individual and think in terms of the country as a whole.

The JWA on the other hand argues for continuity between a private morality and its consistent application in the affairs of state. The present formulation of the JWA has been most often cited when the West was involved in the Falklands War, the Gulf War and to some extent in the conflict in Bosnia. The JWA suggests that wars are intrinsically wrong but, as a last resort, often needed as the lesser of two evils.

Consider the following quotations for what they tell us about war and peace. The realist does not think war is good but just a fact of life. Some such as Clausewitz suggest that war is the way in which governments 'talk' to each other. We can perhaps see how this is happening today in the case of the Gulf War (1990) or more recently in the bombing of Serbian strategic sites by Nato forces to protect the Albanian people living in Kosovo (March, 1999). In both cases military action was being used to reinforce threats by government.

1 We know, certainly, that War is only called forth through the political intercourse of Governments and nations; but in general it is supposed that such intercourse is broken off by War, and that a totally different state of things ensues, subject to no laws but its own. We maintain, on

5 the contrary, that War is nothing but a continuation of political
  intercourse, with a mixture of other means.

K Clausewitz von, On War, 1833 (Penguin edition 1982), p. 402

Walzar considers how the realist reconciles public and private
morality. A ruler decides to torture a terrorist who knows the
whereabouts of a bomb that will, if it explodes, kill hundreds of
innocent people. We recognise that public figures sometimes have to
live in two worlds and our judgements of them do not always allow for
the impossibility of their situations.

1 When he ordered the prisoner to be tortured, he committed a moral
  crime and he accepted a moral burden. Now he is a guilty man. His
  willingness to acknowledge and bear (and perhaps to repent and do
  penance for) his guilt is evidence, and it is the only evidence he can
5 offer us, that he is not too good for politics and that he is good enough.
  Here is the moral politician: it is by his dirty hands that we know him.
  If he were a moral man and nothing else, his hands would not be dirty;
  if he were a politician and nothing else, he would pretend that they
  were clean.

M Walzer quoted by M Cohen et al in War and Moral Responsibility
(Princeton University Press, 1994) pp. 69–70

Finally Cheshire recognises that personal morality cannot exist in
isolation; I have a duty to others which means sacrificing my own
sense of what is ultimately right.

1 If it's myself who is being attacked, it may be a counsel of perfection
  that I turn the other cheek and allow myself to be killed but if the
  aggressor is killing someone else, or worse still, a whole group of
  others, then it cannot be a counsel of perfection for me to refrain from
5 going to their defence ... my clear duty in charity is to defend the victims.

Cheshire L, Where is God in all this? (St Paul Publications, 1991) pp. 72–73

The militarist and pacifist on the other hand place ideals above
situations and personal morality. Ayatollah Khomeini, the Islamic Shi'ite
fundamentalist leader, sees war as an expression of the power and
effectiveness of religion: 'A religion without war is a crippled religion'.

The founding fathers of communism Marx and Engels not only
regarded the need for revolution as a means to establish communism
but also as an expression of what communism stands for: the
overthrow of ruling classes by the workers.

[Revolution is necessary] not only because the *ruling* class cannot be
overthrown in any other way but also because the class *overthrowing* it
can only in a revolution succeed in ridding itself of all the muck of ages
and become fitted to found society anew.

Marx K and Engels F *Collected Works* (Progress, Moscow 1975–90) Vol. 5, p. 53

But the pacifist is no different. By refusing to use any form of violence the pacifist is publicly expressing his beliefs, whatever the consequence. Here is how one Christian pacifist puts it:

> Non-violence is not an option for Christians. It is the essence of the gospel.
>
> W Wink *Is There an Ethic of Violence?* quoted in
> A Coates, *The Ethics of War*, p. 87

2 Realism

The realist view of war is quite often presented, as one might expect, by those who have had first-hand experience of war itself – as combatants or senior politicians. Leonard Cheshire's quotation above represents a view which goes back to Augustine, which makes a distinction that is fundamental to the realist: personal moral perfection is a very different affair from the morality which is necessary in governing a state. Cheshire, like Harris, had served in Bomber Command during the Second World War and they had both experienced the devastation which war brings. For instance after the controversial aerial bombing of German cities such as Dresden and Hamburg, Air Marshal Harris said:

> There was nothing to be ashamed of in the sort of thing that has to be done in every war, as of war itself.
>
> A Harris, *Bomber Offensive* (Greenhall Books, 1990) p. 58

Harris's remark reminds his critics that in war nothing is neat. Strategically and indeed morally his action was justified because it was the enemy who had perpetrated the evil which he had been put in the position of eradicating. Realism does not celebrate war and at no stage does it say that it is intrinsically good. What it claims is that war is a morally justifiable *public* act as part of the process of maintaining law and order. There are many variations of the realist position, but the following are the characteristics of those who advocate some form of *military realism*.

Pacifist utopians (those who believe that humans can achieve a state where there will be no violence and live in cooperation) are accused of *causing* wars by the realist because they insist on consistent private/public moral behaviour. Realists claim that as they are unable to take the necessary strategic or practical steps early enough they in fact cause war. Some realists have called this the 'instrumentality of evil'.

Moral utopians (those who believe that the use of war is a duty to overcome evil) are accused of prolonging wars. Realists point to Vietnam or Somalia or even Bosnia where the use of war on 'humanitarian' and other ideological grounds has resulted in more death and greater confusion. Realists are very wary when countries play the 'moral policeman' and use war as a means to do so.

Wars should be governed primarily by practical ends not moral considerations. Ironically by employing 'objective instrumentality' the realist argues that wars are, in the end, more moral. The case of the Gulf War is an example where military strategists argued for further attacks, but were hindered by public moral concern. As a result, it is argued, the Iraqi issue was never satisfactorily concluded.

Some realists simply accept that there will be an uneasy relationship between private and public morality. Public morality is almost by definition one of compromise. Some Christian theologians such as Reinhold **Niebuhr** (Protestant) argue that all political decisions are prone to sin. This view accepts the hazy relationship between public and private morality but does not reduce the moral duty to act and choose. In a tragic world such decisions become all the more important and Niebuhr recognises that humans cannot make perfect choices. He has little time for Christian pacifists and their 'soft utopias' (see Raven's defence below, pages 117–118).

Other realists give absolute power to the state. The state justifies itself by acting for itself. This creates a form of **moral dualism** that does not attempt to apply personal standards to public affairs but allows the state to act according to its own criteria.

3 Militarism

> **KEY ISSUE** Is there a place for a 'holy war' in Christian doctrine?

The militarist, like the pacifist, is an idealist. Whereas for the pacifist war is intrinsically wrong, for the militarist war is good and inextricably linked to the establishment of the state or the expression of a cause. There is a psychology here which celebrates the virtues which war or terrorism generates, such as loyalty to the fatherland or complete commitment to the cause or utter belief in God. The replacement of people through war, for instance, symbolises the ease with which communism will regenerate itself. It has often been observed that some terrorists and freedom fighters continue their combat even when all is lost or curiously prolong combat when other means are possible because it is the fighting itself which is important not so much the outcome. Without war their identity would be lost.

Militarist war is an end in itself. As A J Coates has argued (*The Ethics of War*, 1997), militarism is not the sole province of fascist dictators but is shared by all across the political and ideological spectrum. Militarism may also to be found in the **holy war** arguments both within Christianity and Islam and is not just confined to the fundamentalist position expressed by Ayatollah Khomeini above. When the motive is a moral crusade, to die for the cause is to die as a martyr and receive its rewards. The enemies are no longer human beings but demonised as representatives of evil. War is not the lesser of two evils, or an instrument of peace, but an outward act of good.

a) Islam

Islam permits the use of military force when Islam is itself under attack or oppression. In mainstream Islamic thought **military** or **lesser jihad** is only possible when legitimised by the ruler in agreement with his senior theologians. Thus the 'struggle' (the meaning of *jihad*) becomes the driving force behind so much fundamentalist Islamic behaviour. For Shia Islam, war of this kind is far from tragic, it is, as Khomeini described it, the 'key to paradise'.

b) Christianity

For centuries Christianity did not have a holy war doctrine. The New Testament is at best ambivalent about the use of violence and until the First Crusade those who fought in battle had to do penance afterwards in order to receive communion and clergymen were forbidden to fight. But in 1095 CE at the Council of Clermont the Pope, Urban II, established the ground rules for a defensive war which rapidly became the basis in the popular mind for Christian holy war. The 'war of religion' was in the first instance to maintain Christian lands, not to expel or annihilate the **infidel**. However, the language used by the Pope stressed the religious virtues of the soldier – they were to be 'soldiers of Christ', their deaths were acts of sacrificial love in the same way as Christ had died for the world. Furthermore, whereas St Paul had described the individual's life in terms of a personal war between sin and the spiritual life (Romans 7:13–25), war was now elevated to the public level as part of the Christian spiritual battle to overcome evil.

> For I delight in the law of God, in my inmost self, but I see in my members another law at war with the law of my mind and making me captive to the law of sin which dwells in my members.
>
> Romans 7:22–23

The soldier was depicted in priestly terms taking vows of penitence and obedience and wearing the cross. As a soldier of Christ he would receive pardon and remission of sins and the promise of life eternal. But if Urban II had intended only to permit a restrained version of religious war, it was, at a popular level, rapidly transformed into a full-blown holy war, where the death of the infidel was sufficient justification for war. Subsequent atrocities and the slaughter of innocent women and children – especially of the Jews (who were accused of Christocide or killing of God's Son, Jesus Christ) – are remembered uneasily today by Christians brought up with a renewed understanding of Christianity's pacifist roots.

c) A moral vision

Driven by a moral vision, the militarist is not restrained by the JWA notion of proportion or the realist's anti-idealism. War is expressive. Burke described the French Revolution as an 'armed doctrine', others have used phrases such as the 'happy warrior' to describe the soldier in war. Eight million have died in the former USSR, one million in Cambodia and one million in Ethiopia as the result of ideological struggles. The *kamikaze* or 'divine wind special attack force' pilots in the Second World War between April and June 1945 destroyed 20 US warships. War of this kind with its scant regard for personal life and utter commitment to the ideal also had the psychological effect of bewildering and terrifying the enemy. It put in stark relief the distinct moral beliefs of each side.

Those who criticise the militarist viewpoint find its central moral position contradictory. War is fought to achieve a state for its citizens to enjoy, and yet such is the 'expressive' power of war, that the state is happy to dispense with its citizens who will never enjoy the fruit of their labours. Militarism is prone to unchecked intensity, escalation and scant regard for non-combatants. It is primarily in responding to these criticisms that the JWA was formulated.

4 Pacifism

KEY ISSUE Is all war intrinsically wrong?

Pacifism as **absolute pacifism** shares the same idealistic outlook as the militarist, the essential difference being that it regards all war as *intrinsically* wrong. The issue for the pacifist, therefore, is not the rights or wrongs of war but the means by which the individual can ensure justice without recourse to violence. However, pacifism may also be taken as a broad term for all those whose **teleological** aim (i.e. who think in terms of a *'telos'* or a final state) is to establish peace whilst acknowledging that the means may, on occasion, require the use of war. Those who take this pragmatic line share some of the realist's reasoning and the JWA desire to keep war to a minimum. **Contingent pacifism** therefore acknowledges that peace is dependent on other factors.

a) Absolute pacifism

In the West absolute pacifism has its origins in the Christian tradition. The picture which emerges of the very early Christians was a group who rigorously practised the teachings of Jesus (see the Sermon on the Mount in Matthew 5:1–48) concerning loving one's enemies, turning the other cheek when wronged, settling disputes out of court, checking anger before it escalated into violence. Paul's letter to the Romans (Romans 12:14–21) indicates just how deeply ingrained this attitude was at a very early stage. **Tertullian** (*c.* 160–220 CE) represents what many regarded at the time as a normative or standard practice of pacifism:

> But how will a Christian man war, nay how will he serve even in peace, without a sword, which the Lord has taken away? The Lord, in disarming Peter, unbelted every soldier.
>
> from Tertullian *On Idolatry* in R Gill, *A Textbook of Christian Ethics* (1995), p. 260

There are several problems which face Christian theologians today: was Jesus' ethic primarily a programme for personal holiness, or was the ethic intended to be extended to society as a whole, or was it simply a description and promise of the eschatological age *yet to come*? In addition, a major problem which faces any pacifist and particularly those who derive their pacifism from a Christian *a priori* is whether a person has a responsibility to the state when their country is engaged in war. For although pacifism may be possible at a personal level the Christian also has a duty to others and to the state (see also pp. 116–118).

b) St Augustine (354–430 CE)

Augustine was clear that pacifism was the hallmark of the Christian's *personal* relationship with others, but it could not be extended wholesale into politics. Those who argue this are more properly **contingent pacifists**. The key notion here is responsibility for innocent lives. Whereas my duty to myself is self-centred and cannot justify force, I have a duty to protect the weak and even, in the image of Christ Himself, lay down my life for others as an act of self-sacrificial love.

> This is my commandment, that you love one another as I have loved you. Greater love has no man than this, that a man lay down his life for his friends.
>
> John 15:12–13

c) Christian eschatology

Christian **eschatology** (the study of the end and the arrival of the Kingdom of God) is a significant factor here. For those Christians who imagine a future, possibly imminent, arrival of the Kingdom of God there is a moral urgency to maintain a standard of holiness which is greater than any ordinary expectation. The peace ideal must be kept at all times. Others argue that the Kingdom is a process which is evolving and developing until the eschaton arrives (final judgement and the return of Christ) and the world achieves its perfection. The end is peace, but this may only come through present struggle: it is an ideal to aspire to. In an imperfect world coercive action may sometimes be necessary.

d) Martin Luther King (1929–68)

King is one of the great advocates of those who understood the Christian vision as a political reality at the personal and social level. His pacifism did not mean (as it is sometimes criticised to mean) inaction, but rather **direct non-violent** action. His language is strongly eschatological and he knew that in the process of change there would be casualties. His own life and death (by assassination) act as an icon for the pacifist movement. Those who support this line of reasoning point to its moral consistency, its sense of moral virtue and the long-term stability achieved through evolutionary change rather than sudden revolution. King's methods are paralleled to **Gandhi**'s (1869–1948) political transformation (through *ahisma* or non-violence) of the working conditions of the 'coloureds' in South Africa and the untouchables in India. Both men employed the use of strikes, sanctions, peaceful protest and civil disobedience.

e) Quakers

The Society of Friends or **Quakers** was founded in part on the principle that violence can only beget violence. The Quaker is encouraged to see the element or spark of God in each person and actively to overcome all that which causes conflict between people. But as this quotation suggests this can never on any account include the use of violence.

1 The Spirit of Christ by which we are guided is not changeable, so as once to command us from a thing as evil, and again to move unto it; and we certainly know, and testify to the world, that the Spirit of Christ, which leads us into all truth, will never move us to fight and war
5 against any man with outward weapons, neither for the kingdom of Christ, nor for the kingdoms of the world.

A Declaration from the Harmless and Innocent People of God called Quakers
presented to Charles II in 1660

f) Contingent pacifism

The contingent pacifist does not share the optimism of the absolute pacifist. While society still contains evil people, then the use of force can sometimes be justifiable. There is no one kind of contingent pacifist. Some argue that war might be used to defend territory or rights, but the use of biological warfare is unacceptable because it cannot be controlled and might cause the death of innocent people. Others describe themselves as **'nuclear pacifists'** for similar reasons. Moreover nuclear war is always disproportionate to any end and could never result in peace in any meaningful way which would satisfy the Christian vision (discussed further in Chapter 7).

There are some contingent pacifists (**war pacifists**) who allow self-defence and yet reject the claim that war is merely an extension of this. War is too impersonal, too broad and uncertain and the individual has no sense of direct moral responsibility which usually accompanies self-defence.

g) The wickedness of pacifism

We have already seen that some forms of pacifism are accused of promoting evil. An important Roman Catholic argument was put forward by the philosopher G E M Anscombe. Her argument depends on the principle that the innocent should always be protected. The only consideration, Anscombe argues, is whether attacking someone would be unjust. 'Murder is the deliberate killing of the innocent whether for its own sake or as a means to some further end.' If this is the case the absolute pacifist has failed to make a basic moral distinction between innocent and wicked people and their failure to stop the wicked means, in effect, that they are promoting wickedness.

1   The right to attack with a view to killing is something that belongs only to rulers and those whom they command to do it. I have argued that it does belong to rulers precisely because of that threat of violent coercion exercised by those in authority which is essential to the
5   existence of human societies.
    Now pacifism teaches people to make no distinction between the shedding of innocent blood and the shedding of any human blood. And in this way pacifism has corrupted enormous numbers of people who will not act according to its tenets. They become convinced that a
10 number of things are wicked which are not; hence, seeing no way of avoiding 'wickedness', they set no limits to it.

from G E M Anscombe, 'War and Murder' in *Nuclear Weapons:
A Catholic Response*, ed. Walter Stein, quoted in M Palmer
Moral Problems (1991), pp. 123–4

5 Just war

KEY ISSUE Is offensive war necessarily unjust?

The main just war propositions are:

- War must be sanctioned by a legitimate authority.
- There must be a just cause (those attacked must deserve it).
- War must be fought with the right intentions (i.e. to achieve peace), be proportionate to the end and calculate success.
- War should be the last resort.
- There must be proportional means in war.
- Non-combatants must be given immunity in war.

The just war argument (JWA) developed in Christian circles as Christians found themselves in positions where their obedience to the state conflicted with their Christian obligation to resist violence. The JWA adopts a number of the elements of the different war attitudes set out above and although much of its history has been in the Christian and **Natural Law** traditions, there is nothing which makes it an *exclusively* Christian argument. It has various forms and has been adapted and added to as warfare, society and differing notions of justice have developed. It originated with Augustine (354–430 CE) who set out the reasons for going to war. Others, notably **Grotius** (1583–1645), applied the Natural Law principle that the innocent (i.e. non-combatants) should have immunity *in war*. The JWA has two distinct but clearly related elements. The *ius ad bellum* (Latin meaning the justification for going to war) established the argument within the context of the state and the *ius in bello* (Latin meaning the just means within war) maintains that war is primarily instrumental and not expressive and must be fought with minimum force to achieve the proper end – peace.

a) Legitimate authority

In the earlier formulations the JWA referred to the sovereign. The sovereign represented God's will on earth and for Augustine this meant the establishment of peace. For Aquinas (c. 1225–74) it ruled out the private citizen. As part of the instrument of government the JWA gave it the right (the Latin legal term is *vis coactiva*) to quash any attempts to overthrow the state or monarch. Today the issue is far from clear. At its most obvious, legitimate authority in the West refers to any democratically elected government, but the international level of many wars in the world today begs the question of what constitutes the relevant body which can authorise the use of military force.

Coates argues that this principle has been largely overlooked with disastrous consequences, resulting in rights being given to terrorists.

More difficult to judge is when an authority is legitimate. What happens if the authorities are not thought to be legitimate? This was a problem which neither Augustine nor Luther resolved satisfactorily. The JWA allows for the internal revolutionary war if the revolutionaries feel that they represent the will of the people, although **Luther** (1483–1546) argued vehemently against the Peasants' Revolt (1524–36) at great cost to his popularity (see pp. 116–117 theological issues). The problem is clearly a difficult one and Aquinas argued that in weighing it up the revolutionary group had to consider whether its action would be in proportion to a possible greater good.

b) Just cause

This part of the JWA is hugely ambiguous. From the first proposition it follows that a legitimate authority may judge what is a 'just cause' which warrants the use of war. But whereas a just cause may be established it is much more philosophically problematic justifying the grounds of war as desert or punishment (see Chapter 5, Killing as Punishment). Furthermore some critics quote a fundamental principle in law, 'let no one be the judge of his own cause'. But who today is politically neutral enough to give objective judgement? Could it be an organisation such as the United Nations? Others argue that the state should take responsibility and accountability for its own actions independently from other nations or organisations.

Much more complicated is what constitutes a just cause. Traditionally the answer appeals to a Natural Law distinction between defence and offence. The principle is enshrined in the much-quoted UN Article 51:

1 Nothing in the present Charter shall impair the inherent right of individual or collective self-defence if an armed attack occurs against a Member of the United Nations, until the Security Council has taken measures necessary to maintain international peace and security.
5 Measures taken by Members in the exercise of this right of self-defence shall be immediately reported to the Security Council and shall not in any way affect the authority and responsibility of the Security Council under the present Charter to take at any time such action as it deems necessary in order to maintain or restore international peace and
10 security.

United Nations Article 51

But is offensive war necessarily unjust? The JWA tries to avoid militarism yet the use of pre-emptive strikes makes moral and strategic sense (Israel justified its pre-emptive attack on Egypt in the Six Day War (1967) on these grounds). What may be perceived as an offensive first strike could also be justified as a response not to *physical* attack but the build up of a *potential* aggressor's troops or provocative behaviour or some kind of interference in the ideology of the defending country.

c) Right intention, or proportionality and recourse to war

The proposition here can be stated in a number of ways. The 'right intention' captures something of the JWA's development in the Natural Law environment of Aquinas. The intention must be for peace – land, rights, protection are not in themselves sufficient grounds for war. Aquinas' version of Natural Law and the feature of the JWA is that the means may be justified as long as they are in proportion to their ends. This is notoriously difficult to determine. How can anyone say before a war, 'Will the outcome justify the reason for going to war?' Bentham's utilitarian calculus (the 'hedonic calculus') is generally thought to be unworkable, and furthermore, even if one could calculate the exact number of dead as a result of a war, would this in itself determine the rightness or wrongness of the war?

The fears of those who warn that technology will always result in total or atomic war have, to some extent, been proved wrong by the technology used in the Gulf War. It illustrates that wars can still be proportionate. Another element which is sometimes included as an *ius in bello* criterion is better included here, and that is the likelihood of success. The Falklands War is a good example of the gamble which the British government took by sending a Task Force half way round the world. To the critics this was a foolish move but with hindsight it was a success. The moral considerations can only be based on the wisdom of the professional soldier.

d) Last resort

The JWA constantly affirms that the aim of war is to establish peace. This criterion therefore checks that other means of settling conflict have been considered and tried. The means employed are those approved by the pacifist (negotiation, sanctions, appeasement). Not surprisingly the sharpest criticism of the JWA is from the pacifist who instinctively feels that all wars can be averted. The problem is again a problem of hindsight. If Churchill had formed an appeasement with Germany in the 1930s, the Second World War may have been averted (Churchill himself acknowledged this). On the other hand many felt that force had been used too hastily in the Gulf War (Russia and France in particular were vocal critics of the USA and UK). A last resort may prove too late and lose the strategic and political advantages while sanctions and negotiations give the enemy time to muster troops. The pacifist does not always take into account the considerable **indiscriminate** suffering and death sanctions cause. The JWA at least aims to be specific and provide the non-combatant with immunity. A last resort need not be the *very* last resort.

e) Proportionality and the conduct of war

Closely related to the use of **proportionality** is the proportionality issue in the *ius in bello* argument part of the JWA. Combat must be conducted justly giving immunity to non-strategic sites, non-combatants and prisoners of war. Most difficult of all is judging how much force to use in battle itself. The celebrated case which illustrates many of these elements is the sinking of the Argentine cruiser the *General Belgrano*.

The *Belgrano* was torpedoed with the loss of 368 Argentine seaman – what makes the case a continued area of controversy is that at the time it was outside the exclusion zone, it seemed to be moving away from the island and Task Force. By way of defence the UK government argued that given the skeleton fleet and its distance from the UK the *Belgrano* posed a possible threat which had they not acted when they did would have had terrible consequences (read Coates, *The Ethics of War*, 1997, pp. 208–14 for a full account of the issues). The Falklands example also raises the question whether loss is to be calculated **unilaterally** or **bilaterally**. The battle of Loos (1915) and the Somme (1916) (where 57,470 men were lost on a single day with little offensive advantage) are two examples where critics question the justification of such action. If the losses have to be put in the context of the whole battle is not the JWA concern for all human life compromised? In the case of the Gulf War the spectacular use of technology reinforced for some the disproportionate use of firepower on the Iraqis. So much depends on the aims and intentions of the war as a whole.

f) Non-combatant immunity

Another cornerstone of the *ius in bello* JWA is the importance laid on the protection of innocent life. Fundamental to all Natural Law arguments is that life is intrinsically valuable. Where war is concerned those who work as an instrument of the state willingly sacrifice their lives but the same cannot be said of non-combatants. The argument in practice is far less clear-cut. Are all non-combatants necessarily innocent? Civilians may be involved in the war effort (making arms, clothes, rations, etc). Perhaps a better term would be that those who are 'harmless' rather than blameless have immunity. But the distinction between harmless and harmful makes the line between combatant and non-combatant very vague and perhaps impossible for the JWA to work properly.

Another major criticism is that whereas the notion of the battlefield in the past was clear-cut, war nowadays is fought over vast areas and often in cities. It is inevitable that non-combatants will suffer. The response to this has been to invoke the double effect (DDE). The double-effect argument can be applied in two ways. First, it might be argued that when choosing a strategic target the *intention* is not to harm non-combatants although there is a likelihood of this happening. The problem here as with any form of the DDE (see pp. 61–62) is that the agent knows, just the same, that innocent lives are at risk. Another form more readily applicable in military terms might be to think of the DDE in terms of 'direct' and 'indirect' consequences. In military terms this helps to decide the moral legitimacy between precision bombing, selective bombing and area bombing. For many only the first is licit because the indirect consequences of the military target, though known, are minimal. But 'targets' do not just have to be military. The horrific 'indirect' results of the area bombing of Hamburg during the Second World War were justified by many as a means of undermining the enemy's morale and bringing a swift end to the war. But is it possible to justify the deaths of 40,000 innocent civilians in a single night? Not to do so is to advocate a form of militarism very alien to the JWA. The problem though remains: how many non-combatant casualties does it take to negate the JWA?

6 Theological issues

A great number of the issues discussed above have their origin in Christian theology and continue to be live issues today. There are, however, many issues which continue to tax the Christian conscience not just in the use of war but also in the Church–state relationship.

a) The Bible

Early on Christian theologians struggled to reconcile the discrepancy between the Old Testament (OT) attitude to war and the New Testament's pacifism. The alternatives are either to reject the Old Testament (as the late first-century heretic Marcion did), to allegorise it, to be very selective or to see it as a stage *before* the revelation of the New Testament. The OT permits offensive war. In Joshua 6 for instance Joshua leads the attack on Jericho as part of his invasion of Canaan. Another important passage referred to by early Christian writers is the killing of the Egyptian soldier by Moses (Exodus 2:11–15) as an act of revenge for abusing a Hebrew slave. By contrast there are many passages in the books of the prophets where the prophet looks forward to a time of peace. Micah, for instance, in his vision of the new Israel, envisages a time of justice, equality and peace:

1 It shall come to pass in the latter days that the mountain of the house of the LORD shall be established as the highest of the mountains. For out of Zion shall go forth the law, and the word of the LORD from Jerusalem. He shall judge between many peoples, and shall decide for
5 strong nations afar off; and they shall beat their swords into ploughshares, and their spears into pruning hooks; nation shall not lift up sword against nation, neither shall they learn war any more; but they shall sit every man under his vine and under his fig tree, and none shall make them afraid; for the mouth of the LORD of hosts has spoken.

Micah 4:1–4

In contrast to the earlier texts which see war as part of Israel's fight for survival and existence, it seems that the pre- and post-exile prophets (before and after 586 BCE) had grown war-weary and whilst not condemning war in itself earnestly hoped that conflict would come to an end and the people could enjoy the covenant with God to the full. It might be argued that Micah's vision is eschatological (i.e. that it considered that this stage of affairs could only happen at some future time). Isaiah's words to the exiles promise peace now:

Speak tenderly to Jerusalem, and cry to her that her warfare is ended, that her iniquity is pardoned, and she has received from the LORD's hand double for all her sins.

Isaiah 40:2

The situation of the New Testament (NT) is very different. It is not one where a nation is either carving out its existence or suffering under attack – although many passages reflect the situation where the Christian believers had to consider their beliefs under Roman rule. The outstanding passage is from Jesus' Sermon on the Mount where the exhortation to love one's enemies marks a decisive shift from the prevailing Graeco-Romano attitude of its day (which was to hate one's enemies):

You have heard that it was said, 'You shall love your neighbour and hate your enemy'. But I say to you, Love your enemies and pray for those who persecute you.

Matthew 5:43

Since there is nothing better or finer than when two people of one heart and mind keep house as man and wife, a grief to their enemies and joy to their friends.

Homer, *Odyssey*, Book 6:185

b) The Church

The Church's position has largely been shaped by two enormously influential positions: that of Augustine's (354–430 CE) Catholic tradition and Luther's (1483–1546) Protestant/reform tradition. Each had the effect of marginalising the Christian pacifist mostly to the minor less influential church traditions (e.g. Quakers (see above under pacifism), Amish, Anabaptists).

i) St Augustine

Augustine (in his *Reply to Faustus the Manichaen, c.* 397 CE) argued that when Moses killed an Egyptian his action was justified (even though it was not legally sanctioned) because it was a preparation for Israel's rebellion against the tyranny of Egypt. Likewise other acts of violence are recorded in the Bible as examples of *private* killing and misplaced virtue. So, for example, in Matthew 26:52–53 Peter cuts off the high priest's servant's ear. Jesus' condemnation of Peter's action, 'Put your sword back into its place; for all who take up the sword shall perish by the sword', is for his hastiness and impetuousness in acting for himself and not at God's command.

The NT and OT are consistent: Moses and Peter both illustrate a desire for *justice* not revenge, or cruelty or lust for power. John the Baptist, for instance (Luke 3:14), did not condemn the soldiers who came to see him because they were warriors, but warned 'Rob no one by violence or by false accusation, and be content with your wages'. Augustine makes much of Jesus' argument from silence. For instance when he cures the Centurion's servant (Matthew 8:8–10) the man is praised for his faith but not condemned for his job as a soldier. And so finally Augustine deals with Jesus' injunctions in Matthew 5. Jesus' teaching is not concerned with a literal physical 'turning of the other cheek' but with an inner disposition of peacemaking – and although this is implicit in the OT it takes the revelation of Jesus to make this promise of the Kingdom of God explicit.

ii) Luther

Luther's argument (*Whether soldiers, too, can be saved,* 1526 CE) depends on his essential distinction between the two kingdoms: the kingdom of this world and the spiritual kingdom to come of the true Christian. At first it seems that a soldier's life is very alien to the life of Christian love. But on reflection, and in a wider context of the good which he achieves, 'I observe that it amputates a leg or hand, so that the whole body may not perish, therefore, such a war is only a very brief lack of peace'. Romans 13:4 justifies the use of the sword as a means through which God carries out his judgement using man. Luther also refers to John the Baptist's words of moral exhortation to the soldiers (Luke 3:14), 'now the abuse does not affect the office'. Even Jesus suggests that war has its place on the earthly plane: 'if my kingship were of this world, my servants would fight' (John 18:36). War cannot be wrong if it is the will of God, because then Moses, Joshua and David would be condemned for using violence. Instead they are praised. The NT sanctions the use of war in obedience to earthly authorities through whom God operates.

> Be subject for the Lord's sake to every human institution, whether it be to the emperor as supreme, or to governors as sent by him to punish those who do wrong and to praise those who do right.
>
> I Peter 2:13–14

c) Tradition and conscience

One of the major factors which has determined the interpretation of biblical texts has been the equally important notion of the Christian's allegiance to the state or ruler. The term used today by pacifists, 'conscientious objector', argues that a Christian's private morality supersedes his obligations to the state. Clearly, if everyone thought this the functioning of the state would become impossible and so the biblical precedent and subsequent Church tradition are of crucial importance. Augustine and Luther both distinguish between the secular realm and the Kingdom of God or Heavenly City (Augustine). The earthly kingdom, though redeemed from the collective guilt of original sin, is tainted by the sinful wills of individuals. In other words Christians may have a vision of what *could* be the case and strive towards it, but they live under secular authority and must learn to compromise. Very early Christians had taken the texts in Mark 12:17 ('Render to Caesar the things which are Caesar's, and to God the things which are God's') and Romans 13:1 ('Let every person be subject to the governing authorities. For there is no authority except from God') to be minimal obligations to state and authority and had avoided military service. The adoption of Christianity by the emperor Constantine posed Augustine particular difficulties which he uneasily resolved through his two-cities model.

By the time of Luther the position is far more clear-cut and he distinguishes clearly between the authority of state and the authority of the Church (a form of theological realism, see pp. 102–103). So, Luther argues in an extreme case, even if the ruler is a tyrant he must be obeyed because he still has reason enough to respond to the will of God. The only grounds for civil war would be against a madman who, because he had lost his reason and ability to respond to God, is no longer able to do good. A Christian's duty is always to the state:

> A tyrant, however, may do things that are far worse than the insane man does, but he still knows that he is doing wrong. He still has a conscience and his faculties. There is the hope that he may improve. We can never hope that an insane man will do this for he is like a clod or

5   a stone. If injustice is to be suffered, then it is better for subjects to
    suffer it from their rulers than for the rulers to suffer it from their
    subjects.

> from Luther, *Whether soldiers, too, can be saved,* quoted in R Gill,
> *A Textbook of Christian Ethics* (1995), pp. 297–8

The issue of loyalty to the state remains unresolved for Christians
today. Whereas in many less crucial issues (arms trade, poll tax,
animal testing, etc.) a democracy allows a Christian the means to
protest without directly affecting whether people die, the refusal to
participate in war inevitably means that others are directly dependent
on your action. This potentially undermines the stability of the state
as Luther feared. Many pacifists, such as Charles **Raven** (1885–1965),
an influential scholar (Regius Professor of Divinity at Cambridge
University) and churchman, risked condemnation from other
Christians by placing conscience before traditional Church teaching
and loyalty to state. His experience of two world wars and the atomic
bombs at Hiroshima and Nagasaki directs his sense of temporal duty
in the first instance to his neighbour not to the state:

1   If we are really prepared under any imaginable circumstances to
    murder the whole population of a hundred square miles by a single
    explosion, it becomes difficult to feel that our churchgoing and prayers,
    our duty toward our neighbours and our talk about love, service and
5   sacrifice can be anything but cant and hypocrisy.

> from Raven, *The Theological Basis of Christian Pacifism* (1952), quoted in
> R Gill, *A Textbook of Christian Ethics* (1985), p. 345

Raven's theology was inspired by the kind of very early Christianity
based on the example of Christ on the cross who had risked
everything as an example for others to imitate. The extract below can
be contrasted not only with Anscombe's criticism of pacifism (see
page 108) but also with the traditional teaching of mainstream
Christianity on loyalty to the state.

1   But in spite of all this compromise and subterfuge the heart of the
    Christian gospel is not safety but victory – the victory over evil that
    was won by the way of the Cross. Jesus, when he undertook his
    mission of deliverance, was constantly tempted to use other methods:
5   the reformer's road of material satisfactions; the statesman's road of
    armed rebellion and imperial rule; the ecclesiastic's road of awe and
    wonder and the fulfilment of prophecy and the role of the Lord's
    anointed. Even at the Mission's crisis in the last days at Jerusalem, he
    could have fled and taken refuge in Galilee. He chose to meet evil
10 unarmed and unafraid, to let it do its worst with him, and to bear its
    wounds in his own body on the tree. So by death came life, and the
    twin sayings – 'I came that they may have life and have it abundantly'

[John 10:10] and 'Whoso loveth his life shall lose it, and whoso hateth
his life in this world shall keep it unto life eternal' [John 12:25] – are
15 seen to be complementary.
    Of course it is possible for us to say that we are incapable of following
his example or else that the example is not one that ought to be
followed. But if in this supreme lesson and achievement we are not to
imitate him, either our discipleship becomes trivial or else his lordship is
20 denied. To say, 'This is too high a price for me to pay', is natural enough,
but we ought surely not to make such a confession without shame. To
say, 'This was right for him, but it would be wrong for me,' is to tear up
those parts of his teaching in which he bade us follow and do his works
and to assume that we can lightly disassociate ourselves from him
25 whenever we think fit. In this matter of victory over evil – a matter
fundamental to his whole ministry – what is not legitimate for us is to
ignore his way or to replace it by some method of our own. But this is
precisely what we do when we call pacifism a soft utopianism or decide
that mass-killing is the lesser of two evils. And if we argue that all action
30 is relative to its particular circumstances and that when Christ stood
before Caiaphas or Pilate he acted in a way quite opposite from what
Christians should take before a Hitler or a Stalin, we ought to support
our disavowal of our Master by strong evidence and with grave hesitation,
else it would seem obvious that we do not take Christ seriously.

from the Robert Treat Paine lectures for 1950,
The Theological Basis of Christian Pacifism, quoted in
R Gill, *A Textbook of Christian Ethics* (1985), pp. 361–2

Answering structured and essay questions

Summary

The following diagram indicates the relationship between different attitudes
to war and peace as the basis for social stability.

1 *War and social order*: war realism, war as instrument of state, war as
    expression of state ideals (utopianism).

2 *Realism*: private v. public morality in war. Criticism of pacifist utopias.

3 *Militarism*: war is expressive of state ideals. Holy war.
    a) Islam: *jihad*
    b) Christianity: crusades
    c) Moral vision

4 *Pacifism*:
    a) Absolute pacifism: war is intrinsically wrong.
    b) St Augustine

c) Christian eschatology
d) Martin Luther King
e) Quakers
f) Contingent pacifism. War pacifism, nuclear pacifism.
g) The wickedness of pacifism. Anscombe's argument.

5 *Theological issues*: this section develops the Christian ideas dealt with briefly above.
a) The Bible
b) Church tradition: Augustine and Luther
c) Tradition and conscience. Charles Raven

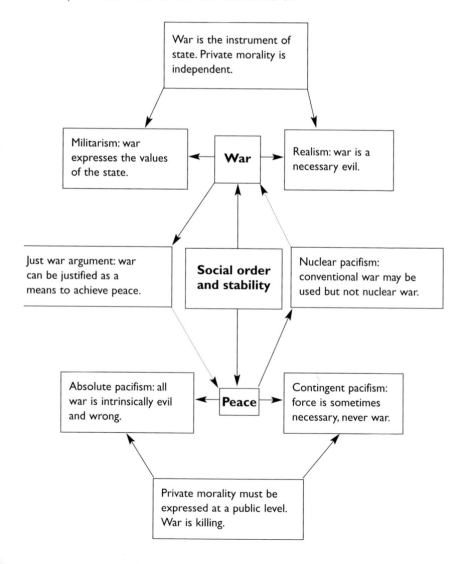

Questions

1a Explain the moral and practical aims of the just war argument.
1b 'The historical circumstances in which the just war argument was first formulated are now so different as to make the argument almost entirely unworkable'. Discuss.
2a Explain the difference between absolute and contingent pacifism.
2b 'A Christian has no choice but to be a pacifist'. Discuss.
3 'In such dangerous things as war the errors which proceed from a spirit of benevolence are the worst' (Clausewitz). What moral considerations, if any, should govern the conduct of war?
4 Is pacifism immoral?
5 Can militarism be defended by Western powers today?
6 Does the just war argument permit a civil war against a violent ruler?

Essay skills

Writing essays on this topic is helped considerably with the knowledge of two or three historical events. In this way you can draw from events to illustrate your arguments. Detailed knowledge of history and long lists of dates are unnecessary; it is the philosophical argument which matters. You could choose from wars such as the Second World War, the Falklands conflict, the Gulf War and civil war in former Yugoslavia/Balkan states. The just war argument is often cited in these cases, but try to be more subtle. Consider whether war is fought for other reasons – is it an expression of democracy, is it for expedience (trade concerns)? Different forms of pacifism should also be distinguished.

Is pacifism immoral?

This essay is about whether more harm might result from a pacifist position than good. Those who criticise pacifism often do so because of its contradictions and irresponsibility. First you should set out the various pacifist positions. Explain the pacifist distinction between coercion and violence. You may then wish to look briefly at the moral motivation for these views. Humanitarian, Christian, reverance for life (Gandhi). Outline the philosophical objections: problems of responsibility for others, a failure to distinguish between the guilty and the innocent. You could contrast Anscombe and Raven arguments. Finally you could consider whether pacifism is legitimate as a private concern but quite different for socieites (analyse Augustine or consider the liberal basis of democracy). On the other hand you could see whether it is an utopian aim or goal for a future but has to be modified by the present corrupt age (contingent pacifism and/or consider the different Christian eschatological interpretations). Conclude.

7 Nuclear War and Deterrence

KEYWORDS

arms race – increase of countries acquiring nuclear weapons

balance of power – political (and nuclear) influence nations have in the world

first strike/second strike – premeditated military action in nuclear war, second strike is the response to an attack by launching a nuclear missile

limited nuclear war – use of nuclear missiles at a tactical level where there is little chance of escalation

MAD – 'Mutually Assured Destruction' i.e. should both sides use nuclear weapons there will be no winners

MIRV – 'multiple independently-targetable re-entry vehicle' – single missile with many warheads to be directed against multiple targets considerable distances apart

multilateral disarmament – reduction in nuclear arsenal done in tandem with other countries to maintain the balance of power

proliferation – build up of nuclear arsenals to maintain effectiveness against enemy attack

tactical/strategic – use of nuclear missiles in the battlefield/at a distance from the enemy's homeland as a last resort

total war – war which does not distinguish combatants from non-combatants, or military from 'soft' targets

Trident/Cruise missiles – Trident: a 'ballistic' missile, i.e. travels outside the earth's atmosphere, launched from a submarine with MIRV. Cruise: travels within the earth's atmosphere, similar to an unmanned aircraft

unilateral disarmament – a country's rejection of nuclear weapons regardless of the policies of other countries

1 Why nuclear weapons?

> **KEY ISSUE** The use of nuclear weapons in war raises a series of quite unique moral and ethical issues which are not necessarily covered in the discussion of **conventional war**. Nuclear missiles shift the arguments primarily because their effects are so much more powerful, quicker, less discriminate and unpredictable.

The use of a nuclear missile provides the means of devastation in war which could only be equalled in conventional terms by vast increases in manpower and bomb capacity. A single one megaton bomb, dropped by a single plane, could do the work of a million V-1 or V-2 bombs used in the Second World War and without the same risk to one's own troops and civilians (see Table 6). The cost and efficiency of nuclear weapons justify huge capital investment to offset what would be needed to support a conventional army with the same firepower capacity.

Table 6 Conventional and nuclear bomb yields

- V-1 and V-2 bombs used by the Germans in the Second World War had yields just under one ton.
- The nuclear bombs used at Hiroshima and Nagasaki in 1945 had yields of 12.5 and 22 kilotons (thousand tons of TNT).
- Nuclear bombs can now be of several megatons. The USSR tested a bomb in 1961 of 56 megatons (million tons of TNT).
- Some nuclear bombs for tactical purposes can have yields as little as 100 tons (0.1 kt).
- Modern weapons have MIRV capacity, that is the ability to place on one missile many warheads which can be targeted to quite separate locations at great distances apart.

Such an attractive means of protecting a country's interests has subsequently led to an **arms race**. Each country has developed bigger capacity bombs and **proliferated** the number of missiles in its possession so that should the enemy destroy one nuclear strategic arsenal it still has others at its disposal. (Argentina, Brazil, China, Egypt, France, India, Iran, Iraq, Israel, N Korea, Pakistan, Russia, S Africa, S Korea, Syria, UK and USA have all developed their nuclear weapon capacity.)

Finally, nuclear weapons have come to be **symbolic**, almost in militarist terms, of a nation's independence and self-sufficiency. The period of the **Cold War** (the threat of invasion of the West from the communist East by the USSR) justified the increase and **proliferation** of nuclear missiles under a US **hegemony** to protect democracy against communism. Britain's nuclear capacity, for instance, was both a contribution to the US defence policy but equally a continuation of the idea that Britain was still a world power (for further discussion read *The Church and the Bomb*, 1982, ch. 2).

a) The moral problems

There are three key related ethical issues which become particularly critical in the context of nuclear deterrence/war. These are **threats**, **bluffs** and **intentions**. Imagine your response to each of the following situations:

- A burglar has just entered your house and is about to steal your video recorder. You point your shotgun at him and threaten to shoot him unless he leaves.
- A headmistress threatens to beat the whole class of lazy pupils if any of them gets less than half marks in school examinations. Privately she knows she would not do so.
- A landlord threatens to kidnap a tenant's wife and children unless he pays the rent due to him.

In which of the cases above is the use of threats morally justified? Are 'bluffs' morally any better or worse than threats? Having promised by way of a threat to shoot or kidnap, is one morally bound to carry out the threat, even if it has bad consequences?

At a trivial level these raise problems which can be reversed or repaired. But in the context of nuclear weaponry where the outcomes are potentially vast, these are not trivial issues and indeed have become the basis of national and international policy.

b) Nuclear destruction

In 1945 two bombs were dropped on the Japanese cities of Hiroshima and Nagasaki. The Second World War was finally brought to an end and Europe could then begin the process of rebuilding its economy. The effects of the bombs were immediately obvious and terrifying in themselves. But it is only in the years following that we have been able to gauge the long-term consequences, because at the time the effects of **fall-out** had not been fully realised or anticipated. For instance, 140,000 were killed at Hiroshima on 6 August, 1945, but in 1978 alone another 2,000 died from the radiation effects of the bomb. Hiroshima and Nagasaki are the *only* time, so far, when nuclear bombs have been used in warfare. Any predictions for the future for the way in which nuclear weapons will work, can only be based on this event and on guesswork (through computer modelling for instance).

Table 7 Effects of a fission nuclear weapon exploding above ground at less than 10,000 feet

Explosion process	Environmental effects	Time
Blast and shock: 50%	collapse of buildings, rupture of eardrums, haemorrhaging of lungs; earth tremors	first minute
Heat and light: 35%	burns, fires caused; excessive heat of tens of millions of degrees centigrade	first few seconds
Initial radiation: 5%	1 megaton bomb causes radioactive cloud rising 11 miles (cigar-shaped, mainly down wind)	24 hours
Residual radiation and fall-out: 10% (delayed)	somatic (i.e. to body) harm to tissues, radiation sickness, cancer death, abortions; genetic (germ line) defects in subsequent children	after 24 hours, world-wide, and for 30–40 years subsequently
EMP	blackout of communication through electro-magnetic interference	

Example: 1 megaton air burst over a city of 4 million people (such as Detroit). 470,000 people killed instantly, 630,000 injured. In addition the long-term effects of radiation have to be taken into account and the likelihood of several targets being bombed at once. Casualties should be reckoned in tens of millions.

Source: Based on *The Church and the Bomb*, Chapter 1, (1982)

What makes the situation different from 50 years ago is that technology has developed a vast array of missiles, each designed to outwit the enemy. The result of this is that we also realise, for the first time, that we have the capacity to destroy ourselves and do irrevocable damage to the world in general. The threat of the Cold War in the late 1980s may have diminished and the USA and the Russian confederacy may have greatly reduced their nuclear capacity, but we should be clear that the threat of nuclear war is still a strong possibility somewhere in the world and will affect us all. The issue is consequently a key political issue on which the **balance of power** between countries depends. (Any reduction of missiles will depend on each country working together **multilaterally** to maintain the present balance of power.) The issues are complicated by the political context of all the moral, philosophical and theological considerations.

2 Just war and nuclear means

KEY ISSUE Is the just war argument unworkable in a nuclear age?

As Table 7 above indicates not all nuclear missiles are the same. They vary according to impact and method. As technology improves (as illustrated in the Gulf War) there is an increasingly high chance that a missile will hit the designated target. All these factors are crucial in considering whether a nuclear missile could be used according to the just war argument (see pp. 109–113 for a fuller analysis of the JWA). The JWA propositions are:

- War must be sanctioned by a legitimate authority.
- There must be a just cause (those attacked must deserve it).
- War must be fought with the right intentions (i.e. to achieve peace), be proportionate to the end and calculate the chances of success.
- War should be the last resort.
- There must be proportional means in war.
- Non-combatants must be given immunity in war.

The two major moral and tactical (i.e. practical) issues which nuclear missiles pose are those of **proportion** and **deterrence**. Within these two categories the other elements of the JWA become apparent: i.e. good intentions and success, non-combatant immunity.

a) Proportion

The first consideration is whether nuclear missiles could be proportionate *ius in bello* (justice within war). This could equally apply to other non-conventional methods, i.e. chemical and biological warfare. A **tactical** warhead used in the theatre of war might be used against a military objective. Its tonnage could be calculated to inflict enough damage to reduce enemy morale sufficiently to bring about capitulation. This, it will be remembered, was the aim of Harris's controversial reasons for the use of conventional bombing on Dresden and Hamburg (see pp. 102, 113). The purpose in using nuclear weapons might be:

- cost and reduction of military personnel;
- speed (i.e. reaction time to the threat);
- psychological effect: demoralising effects caused by the horror of nuclear burns etc.;
- deterrent: a display and warning of military superiority.

i) Arguments against a limited use of nuclear weapons

- **Escalation:** the major fear is that the enemy would retaliate with a larger bomb with less discrimination for non-combatant immunity. This might eventually develop into a full-scale **nuclear war** (see below).
- No use of nuclear (chemical or biological) warfare is sufficiently discriminating ever to be proportionate. The Chernobyl disaster (in 1986) illustrates how even a small amount of radiation can affect animals and humans thousands of miles away and for some considerable

time to come. The UN estimated that 50,000 babies died prematurely between 1946 and 1976 because of the fall-out and genetic damage caused from the *testing* of nuclear bombs. If a nuclear bomb is used in anger the results are simply too long-term and horrendous to be considered even on a limited scale.

● Deterrence is an unstable factor especially in war. There is no guarantee that the enemy will respond favourably. Deterrence worked in Hiroshima, but Japan had no nuclear means of its own to retaliate. Some writers, such as Richard Harries, argue that in general the principle is **'robust'** (*Christianity and War in a Nuclear Age*, 1986, p. 129) because it would not ultimately be in the best interests of either side to let war escalate to a state of total annihilation. This forms part of a more general argument on deterrence *before* military engagement.

It can be seen that the counter-arguments for the limited use of nuclear weapons in the battlefield (or 'theatre of war') force the issue back a stage to consider whether nuclear missiles would always be disproportionate in nuclear war. Nuclear war is a woolly term. In conventional terms 'war' not only suggests a preparation time (during which the propositions *ius ad bellum* can be weighed up) but a period in which the war is fought (allowing for tactical changes, reconsideration of enemy moves, deployment of troops). But in nuclear war the two elements are merged into one – the time differential between firing a **strategic** missile and hitting a target could be between a few seconds and a few minutes. Means and ends are inextricably fused into one. This is one reason why the JWA may not be entirely applicable in its traditional form.

Should this matter? A vitally important part of the JWA derived from its Natural Law roots is that the intentional killing of the innocent is morally reprehensible. But in nuclear war where the intention is to use sufficient force to bring about a conclusion without further engagement the distinction between combatant and non-combatant is very hazy. The term **total war** is often used in this context to refer to the lack of discrimination between military and civilian targets. Could a modified JWA permit nuclear/total war?

ii) Modified just war argument and nuclear war

● The JWA considers the *total* loss of life from all sides. Although there may be considerable loss of civilian life, even so this might be less than if conventional war was to be fought over a long period of time. One also should not forget that psychological damage in conventional war/conflict can last for a very long time (the Northern Ireland conflict for instance remembers the Glorious Revolution in the seventeenth century).

● All cities (i.e. areas occupied by civilians as well as combatants or 'soft targets') have to be treated as potentially hostile otherwise these might act as a human shield and give tactical advantage to the enemy.

- The alternatives might be hard to countenance. The prospect of an extremely murderous and anti-liberal regime could suggest that there is nothing to lose. In this case it might be the best bet to use a **first strike** tactic.
- Is escalation necessarily inevitable? Once the enemy sees the devastation of one nuclear bomb, might they be forced to realise that there is nothing to gain by continuing the conflict? Success is not inevitably ruled out in nuclear war.

iii) Arguments against nuclear war on grounds of proportion

- There are no winners. In the worst possible scenario any number of countries might have been drawn into the conflict and used their nuclear missiles. The inevitability of escalation would result in **MAD – mutually assured destruction**. Even in a far less serious situation the effects of nuclear fall-out, the severe effects on social structures, the devastation to the environment would still be sufficiently terrible always to be disproportionate.
- 'Armageddon': some people have fondly believed in a 'big whoosh' notion that the scale of things will be so enormous that it will, in effect, mark the end of the world. They take some comfort in this fatalistic view of the inevitable outcome of nuclear war. This is highly unlikely; the prospects are more probably a long-drawn-out affair with considerable suffering and uncertainty.
- 'Better red than dead': even life under an evil dictatorship would be better than a world devastated by nuclear war.
- The intentional and indiscriminate killing of non-combatants is morally evil. It is intriguing how persistent that argument is outside either the Natural Law or Christian *a priori*. The nuclear issue has forced a shift in emphasis in recent years from counter-force justifications to considerations of **counter-value**. Whereas some loss of civilian life is anticipated in conventional JWA (as an unfortunate side-effect) the scale of nuclear war suggests that there would be an actual intention to kill. Some attempt has been offered by those who try to defend nuclear war by using the double-effect argument. But it is highly questionable whether it is possible to justify such massive destruction of civilians as *unintended* side-effects of strategic missiles. If there was and is moral outrage caused by the Dresden affair then *a fortiori* (so much more so) nuclear war.

b) Deterrence

For many of the reasons stated above, the JWA does not support the use of nuclear weapons. Paradoxically it is because the end is so awful that the purchase, development and deployment of nuclear missiles are justified because they maintain peace without recourse to war. The MAD (mutually assured destruction) argument suggests that rational self-interest prohibits not only the use of nuclear weapons but also curtails resort to conventional war. In other words both sides depend on the **deterrent effect** of nuclear weapons to keep the peace. The argument is hardly new. Maintaining conventional armies is often justified because of their deterrent symbolism and an argument has been presented above for the use of limited nuclear weapons in war as a threat or a deterrent. The argument here falls into two parts:

- **Empirical/political justification**: since the end of the Second World War the nuclear deterrent has maintained peace or at least prevented wars from escalating. Whether we like it or not the political balance of power historically has come to rely on the nuclear deterrent. Is **unilateral** disarmament desirable or possible?
- **Moral justification**: is it right to keep and maintain weapons of mass destruction even though there may be no intention of using them (the 'bluff' argument)?

The tension between the two parts illustrates the uneasy alliance between public and private morality. The realist argument (see pp. 102–103) cannot work in isolation and although successive governments in the UK have adopted the deterrent position, public morality, pressure groups (such as the Campaign for Nuclear Disarmament) and the collapse of the Cold War in the late 1980s have resulted in a major shift of public attitudes. Is there still a 'logic of deterrence' which can justify the *possession* of nuclear missiles?

i) Utilitarian defence

Utilitarianism has no fundamental objections to the bluff argument. If, by pretending that nuclear weapons will be used in conflict when in fact there is no such intention, war is averted so much the better. The Utilitarian is not so much interested in intentions as outcome and so would support government practice of maintaining nuclear weapons as deterrence. The problem though is how far and to what extent the bluff can be maintained. As far as the public is concerned the government would have to persuade them that they *would* fully intend to use the weapons in the last resort. All those who develop and maintain and all those who train to use nuclear weapons would have to do so fully believing that they might, one day, be used in anger. Clearly there would be no deterrent effect if a potential enemy thought the government was not utterly serious.

There are, of course, practical problems. Can a government sustain a deception of this magnitude? How does it react to potential enemies with nuclear capability? The Cuban missile crisis of 1962 is often cited as the positive aspect of the deterrent defence. Undoubtedly the possession of nuclear weapons on both sides brought the American and the USSR presidents (Kennedy and Khrushchev) to the negotiating table and secured a peaceful and non-violent agreement. It is understandable that for pragmatic reasons policy has depended on a trade-off defence which is prepared to cope with the inconsistencies of deterrence against the increased likelihood of war.

ii) Natural Law defence

The line taken here is based on the proposition that an action is morally right provided it is based on good intentions. The issue here is whether a *counter-value* argument of deterrence can coherently support the intention by *threatening* to use nuclear weapons in order to dissuade potential aggressors. All traditions of Natural Law and most Christian traditions condemn the intention to kill an innocent life – even if good should come of it (e.g. St Paul in Romans 3:8ff). It is simply not possible to intend to deter if it means being prepared to use nuclear force as a very last resort, unless there is some justification for evil will. An evil will, though, creates an evil character, which in this argument would condemn a whole nation.

The argument is by no means clear-cut. Some argue that as deterrence seems to work, then I can genuinely will the usage of nuclear weapons *as* and only as a deterrence – even though I maintain the bluff (see the utilitarian argument above). Some have argued for two kinds of intention (as a variation of the double effect). **Unconditional intention** covers the primary cause to deter from war. **Conditional intention** is the secondary aim to wage war. This, it is claimed, makes it possible to will deterrence without the need to lie or bluff, because the secondary claim is contingent on the first, not the other way round.

John Haldane argues that the *logic* of this kind of argument does not commit me to carrying out my intention when the situation arises ('Defence, Deterrence and the Taking of Life, in Bauckham and Elford, 1989, p. 143). Supposing there was a significant change in circumstances, i.e. an aggressor *has* fired their first missile, there would be no reason why I should be held to my earlier intention which, when I made it, was not based on the possibility of an *actual* nuclear attack. I could, therefore, quite coherently justify a reassessment of my intentions. This conclusion, as it turns out, is not dissimilar to Nato's **flexible response** principle or 'doctrine' (1967) which encourages members to use mixed means (conventional and/or nuclear) as the situation develops.

iii) Nested intentions defence

Gordon Graham has developed what is sometimes termed **nested intentions**. That is where one intention depends on the other. So, as in Haldane's case above, if situations change, I can legitimately alter intentions when other intentions change. In this case the holding of nuclear weapons can be morally justified because the intention is to deter even though this might be 'nested' in terms of actual use. The metaphor being used is that of a set of tables which fit or nest inside each other. So intending to use weapons is in the first sense (like the smallest table inside the nest) part of a greater intention to achieve peace (the present outside table). Once the threat fails, I am now left in the situation where I would actually have to use the weapons (as if the outside table had now been removed). The aim now would be to bring about revenge (which is the next table down, now on the outside). By nesting my intentions I can explain that deterrence applies to one possible situation which is not inconsistent with the actual use of nuclear weapons. The argument is a variation of Haldane's argument above.

1   Different intentions need not be exclusive. For example, I can intend to catch the train at four, and I can intend to visit my aunt in hospital. Not only are these not mutually exclusive, but the former can be part of the latter. I can intend to catch the train as part of my intention to visit my
5   aunt. Now, when it is said that it is wrong to intend to do what it would be wrong to do, it is assumed that 'to do' describes the same action. There may be nothing incorrect in this assumption, but it is inclined to mislead us when we are thinking about deterrence, because the intention I have when I threaten someone, may be nested in a quite
10 different intention from that which I would have were I to carry out my threat. If so, it is possible that the higher intention when I threaten is different to that were I to carry out the threat, and of a different moral order.

    To see this we have to think about the intention within which the
15 threat posed by nuclear deterrence is nested. When I threaten to use nuclear weapons, it is true that I intend to use them. But this is not the proper overall description of my intention. How could this be? My purpose is precisely *not* to have to use the weapons; my intention is to preserve peace, and this is a morally laudable intention. Should
20 deterrence fail, and I use the weapons, my intention in using them could no longer be to preserve peace but, for instance, to retaliate or exact revenge. Retaliation at the cost of thousands of innocent lives, let us agree with the Just War theorist, would be morally deplorable. But now we have a morally significant difference between the threat and the use
25 of nuclear weapons. To threaten to use them as part of a policy of deterrence has the intention of *protecting* innocent lives; their use has the intention of *taking* them. It is only if we fail to take into account the higher level intentions within which the intention to use nuclear weapons is nested (preserving peace versus exacting revenge), that we
30 could think of the role of nuclear weapons in deterrence as no less culpable than their use in war.

G Graham, Ethics and International Relations (1997), p. 87

3 Theological considerations

> **KEY ISSUE** What guidance, if any, does the New Testament offer about the nuclear age?

A number of the considerations set out above already include the responses of theologians. For many theologians responses can only be made based on current secular thinking, and in a situation as novel and critical as nuclear war and deterrence biblical and Church tradition can only provide partial answers.

a) Reason and conscience

For many Christians reason and conscience allow a healthy dialogue between the principles of Christianity (in this case a total rejection of the death by deliberate killing of innocent people) and the facts as they stand in the world. A good example of this way of thinking can be seen in the method and conclusions of *The Church and the Bomb* (1982). Having assessed all current information and secular moral thinking the report concludes:

> 1   For reasons which we have tried to spell out at various points we consider that the nuclear element in deterrence is no longer a reliable or morally acceptable approach to the future of the world. This judgement is reinforced by the fact that an integral part of deterrence
> 5   in practice is crisis management, which may mean in effect going to the brink while relying on fallible human judgement, operating under tremendous stress, to see you through. Given all these considerations, we believe that a nuclear component in deterrence is not sufficiently compelling to outweigh the huge moral imperatives against using
> 10 nuclear weapons at all.
>
> *The Church and the Bomb* (1982), p. 154

The report's conclusion marked a significant shift in current Church thinking. The Methodist Conference in 1983 was more decisive and proposed unilateral disarmament.

b) Doctrine

Some theologians have tackled the issue from the Christian understanding of God's relationship with the world and human history.

i) Judgement

Those who hold a strong providential view of God's action in the world even suggest that the inevitability of nuclear war and its effects on the world is part of God's plan, a final judgement which will mark the end of the present age. Mark 13:14–27 gives a graphic description of the world after wars and terrible destruction caused by man:

> But in those days, after that tribulation, the sun will be darkened, the moon will not give its light ... the powers in heaven will be shaken. And then they will see the Son of Man coming in clouds with great power and glory.

In 1958 the Archbishop of Canterbury, Dr Fisher, argued that nuclear war and world catastrophe might even be the means by which God would bring this age to an end and from which man's final redemption after judgement could take place. The essay, understandably, caused great furore (see under biblical interpretation below).

ii) Atonement

Other theologians take the doctrine of the atonement as a starting point, and concentrate on the sacrifice and suffering of Christ to bring all people to Him through reconciliation (e.g. see 2 Corinthians 5:18–21). If this is potentially risky the Christian who adopts this as a justification for unilateralism takes the example of the risk God takes in the incarnation and Jesus' own life and suffering for others.

iii) Creation

Alternatively some start with the Christian doctrine of creation. In Genesis 1:27 God gives humans the responsibility to look after the whole planet. The effects of nuclear war, it is argued, would so decimate the world (not just human life, but all levels of creation) that no possible justification could warrant unleashing such destructive forces. God's love for His creation is re-expressed through the incarnation, and it must be this quality which humans apply not only to one another but to creation itself. Again this does not rule out all uses of nuclear weapons; some theologians have suggested that limited nuclear war is consistent with man's freedom to steward the world.

c) Biblical interpretation

In addition to the biblical texts used in the arguments above, one area of particular concern relates to Jesus' understanding of the end, the **eschatological** age to come. The issue of nuclear war, more than any other moral issue, questions to what extent the Christian lifestyle is preparation for the age to come (the passive view) or the establishment of the Kingdom now (the active view).

i) The passive view of the end

The passive view has already been referred to briefly above with Dr Fisher's controversial argument in the late 1950s. The passive view argues that although Jesus anticipated an imminent end of the present age, He was ambiguous (or mistaken) about when it would actually occur. Jesus may have been deliberately uncertain about His prophecies about the end:

> Watch therefore, for you do not know on what day your Lord is coming.

> Matthew 24:42

Perhaps He was ambiguous so that Christians have a duty to be constantly spiritually prepared for the end whenever that might be. The Christian community at Thessalonica, for instance, anticipated an early end and had to be corrected by St Paul when he wrote to remind them of the signs which would first have to precede the end (e.g. 'The coming of the lawless one by the activity of Satan' 2 Thessalonians 2:9).

The book of Revelation provides more conservative theologians with a timescale in which these things will come to pass ('And when the thousand years are ended, Satan will be loosed from his prison' Revelation 29:7), although there are still enormous difficulties tying these prophecies in with actual history. The result is that Christians must, like the five wise girls in Jesus' parable (Matthew 25:1–13), be constantly prepared by living a life of moral and spiritual purity until the second coming of Jesus (the Parousia) and **final judgement**. The NT read in this way encourages the Christian to see Jesus' prophecy of catastrophe, judgement and the new age as the motivation for proselytising (converting) others to become Christian, but with no direct moral imperative to avert world powers from the use of nuclear weapons.

ii) The active view of the end

NT scholars who adopt the **active view**, on the other hand, do so because in general they feel that Jesus' teaching of the Kingdom suggested that it had already *begun* in his lifetime. For example, 'If it is by the finger of God that I cast out demons, then the Kingdom of God has come upon you' (Luke 11:20) or 'Jesus came into Galilee, preaching the gospel of God, and saying, "The time is fulfilled, and the Kingdom of God is at hand, repent and believe in the gospel"'(Mark 1:14–15). In other words, Jesus' own lifestyle and activity are not simply those of a prophet who warns about the coming catastrophe, but a man with a vision of God wanting to establish a new community and combat evil *now*. The Christian, therefore, is encouraged to build communities based on love (John 15:9 the image of the vine), cooperate with enemies (Matthew 5:43; Romans 12:14), struggle for peace and justice (Matthew 5:1–12, the Beatitudes) and, inspired by the renewing presence of the Spirit, seek to avert catastrophe ('In the world you have tribulations; but be of good cheer, I have overcome the world', John 16:33, see also 2 Corinthians 5:17).

Recent studies of apocalyptic (literally 'revelatory') literature have added considerably to this interpretation. Christopher Rowland (*Christian Origins*, 1985) has argued that apocalyptic literature is not just about giving a detailed plan of future catastrophe but a hopeful vision (*Christian Origins*, p. 177) of how things could be developing *now* as the prophet sees them perfectly set out in heaven. So, in the book of Revelation the author describes his vision of heaven where the Lamb's blood (the heavenly Jesus) cleanses the world from sin and a court of the heavenly saints depicts the community redeemed and in harmony.

> Behold, a great multitude which no man could number, from every nation, standing before the Lamb, clothed in white robes, with palm branches in their hands.
>
> Revelation 7:9

The metaphor of 'Armageddon' (the final catastrophic battle between the kings of the world, e.g. Revelation 16:16) is not just a prophecy of what *will* happen but a vision of the evil which the Christian must also resist (Revelation 3:12) in the process of salvation begun and continued by Christ (*Christian Origins*, p. 253). In other words, an inaugurated eschatology leaves no place for complacency, fatalism or introverted morality. The Christian, if he or she understands the NT in this way, has a duty to resist any form of evil and world catastrophe as their role in the process by which the Kingdom becomes a reality on earth.

Understanding the eschatological dimensions of the NT presents the Christian with a major problem of ethical interpretation. It is no wonder then that later Christian traditions have continued to present such diverse views. Rowland concludes:

> Until we take seriously the way in which early Christian writers came to a compromise between their eschatological convictions, realised and future, and their belief that their new lord did not mean separation from the world, we shall not understand a fundamental element of the dynamic of early Christian religion.
>
> C Rowland, *Christian Origins* (1991), p. 283

Answering structured and essay questions

Summary

The following diagram indicates the relationship between different attitudes to war and peace as the basis for social stability.

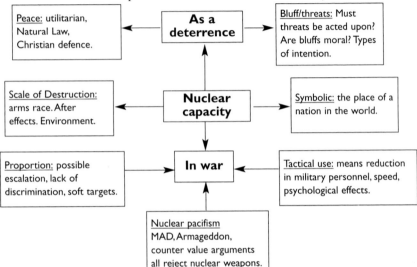

1 *Nuclear weapons*: symbols of power.

    a)   Moral problems: threats, and bluffs.

    b)   Nuclear destruction: effects of nuclear bombs. Balance of power.

2 *Just war and nuclear means*: Two elements of the JWA are considered:

    a)   Proportion: arguments for use of nuclear warheads in war.

        (i)   Arguments against limited use: the problem of escalation, discrimination and total war.

        (ii)   Modified just war argument: best bet and first strike.

        (iii)   Arguments against nuclear war on grounds of proportion: MAD, counter-value arguments.

    b)   Deterrence:

        (i)   Utilitarian defence: trade-off.

        (ii)   Natural Law defence: evil will, bluff. Conditional and unconditional intention.

        (iii)   Nested intentions defence.

3 *Theological considerations*:

    a)   Reason and conscience. Church of England report.

    b)   Doctrine: judgement, atonement, creation.

    c)   Biblical interpretations: passive views of the end, active views of the end.

Questions

1a Explain the moral arguments for and against having nuclear missiles as a form of deterrence.

1b Discuss in what circumstances, if any, the use of nuclear weapons can be morally justified.

2a Explain why a limited nuclear war might be better than the use of conventional war.

2b Assess the view that threatening to use nuclear weapons is morally wrong.

3 'Why not do evil that good may come?' (Romans 3:8). Is there a coherent Christian argument to support nuclear deterrence?

4 Is the just war argument unworkable in a nuclear age? Discuss and give reasons for your answer.

5 'Unilateral nuclear disarmament is the only possible Christian option.' Assess the arguments which support this statement.

6 'The atom bomb is nothing to be afraid of. China has many people. They cannot be bombed out of existence. If someone else can drop an atomic bomb, I can too. The death of ten or twenty million people is nothing to be afraid of' (Chairman Mao, 1957). Discuss whether MAD (mutually assured destruction) as a principle of nuclear deterrence is morally and tactically acceptable.

7 What guidance, if any, does the New Testament offer Christians in their deliberations about nuclear deterrence?

Essay skills

Many essays on this topic have been posed within the just war tradition. Rather than considering all the propositions it is best to consider one or two thoroughly. This chapter has focused on proportion. Make sure you justify which propositions you have selected. The other area of discussion is that of deterrence. It is important here that you consider the balance between good intentions, evil intentions and outcomes. Some technical knowledge is useful, but essays are not testing this kind of knowledge. Knowledge of Hiroshima and Nagasaki and the Cuban missiles crisis help to provide some concrete examples.

Is the just war argument unworkable in a nuclear age? Discuss and give reasons for your answer.

This essay is a very standard one. It is worth outlining the main elements of the JWA. Indicate the two elements of the JWA between *ius in bello* and *ius ad bellum*. You might then go on to consider to what degree the prospect of nuclear attack modifies the argument. Analyse the just war emphasis on proportion. Consider proportion in terms of moral (innocent lives, soft targets, 'cities') and strategic (first strike) terms. In your conclusion you could point out that a nuclear age does not necessarily mean that nuclear weapons have to be used.

Bibliography

Abortion and the Church: What are the Issues? (Church House Publishing, 1993)

Abortion: an Ethical Discussion (Church House Publishing, 1965)

A. Alvarez *The Savage God: A Study of Suicide* (Penguin, 1974)

Amnesty International *When the State Kills...* (Amnesty International Publications, 1989)

T. Aquinas *Summa Theologiae, a Concise Translation* (trans. McDermott. Methuen, 1989)

Augustine *City of God* (trans. Knowles. Penguin, 1972)

R. Bauckham and R. Elford (editors) *The Nuclear Weapons Debate: Theological and Ethincal Issues* (SCM 1989)

T. Beauchamp and J. Childress *Principles of Biomedical Ethics* (Oxford University Press, 4th edition 1994).

D. Brown *Choices: Ethics and the Christian* (Blackwell, 1983).

A. Camus *The Myth of Sisyphus* (trans. O'Brien. Penguin 1975)

E. Carrit *Ethical and Polital Thinking* (Oxford University Press, 1947)

Catechism of the Catholic Church (English translation. Chapman, 1994)

M. Charlesworth *Bioethics in a Liberal Society* (Cambridge University Press, 1993)

A. Coates *The Ethics of War* (Manchester University Press, 1997)

R. Dworkin, *Life's Dominion* (HarperCollins, 1993)

J. Fletcher *Situationism* (Westminster John Knox Press, 1966)

A. Gide, *The Vatican Cellars* (trans. D. Bussy. Penguin, 1969)

R. Gill *A Textbook of Christian Ethics* (T&T Clark, 1985, 1995)

J. Glover *Causing Death and Saving Lives* (Penguin, 1977)

G. Graham *Ethics and International Relations* (Blackwell, 1997)

B. Häring *Medical Ethics* (St Pauls 3rd ed., 1991)

R. Harries *Christianity and War in a Nuclear Age* (Mowbray, 1986)

J. Harris *The Value of Life: An Introduction to Medical Ethics* (Routledge, 1985)

T. Honderich *Punishment: The Supposed Justifications* (Penguin reissue with new postscript, 1984; Polity Press 1989)

D. Hume *On Suicide* (in Singer *Applied Ethics* Oxford University Press, 1986)

R. Jones *Groundwork of Christian Ethics* (Epworth, 1984)

I. Kant *The Grounding for the Metaphysics of Morals* (trans. Elington. Hackett 1981)

J. Kilner N. Cameron, D. Schiedermayer (eds.) Bioethics and the future of medicine: A Christian Appraisal (Eerdmans, 1995)

A. MacIntyre *A Short History of Ethics* (RKP 1967)

Medical Ethics Today (British Medical Association, 1993)

J. S. Mill *On Liberty* (in *Utilitarianism* ed. Warnock. Fount, 1962)

M. Palmer *Moral Problems* (Lutterworth, 1991)

G. Pence *Classic Cases in Medical Ethics* (McGraw-Hill 2nd edition, 1995).

Plato *Phaedo* (Penguin 1989 *The Last Days of Socrates*, trans.
    H. Tredermick)
L. Pojman and J. Reiman *The Death Penalty: For and Against*
    (Rowman & Littlefield, 1998)
H. Potter *Hanging in Judgement: Religion and the Death Penalty in
    England from the Bloody Code to Abolition* (SCM, 1993)
H. Prejean *Dead Man Walking: An Eyewitness Account of the Death
    Penalty in the United States* (HarperCollins, 1996)
Rights and Responsibilities of Doctors (British Medical Association, 1992).
C. Rowland *Christian Origins* (SPCK 1985, 1991)
J-P, Sartre *Existentialism and Humanism* (trans. P. Mairet in
    Methuen 1948)
P. Singer *Rethinking Life and Death* (Oxford University Press, 1995)
P. Singer *Practical Ethics* (Cambridge University Press, 1979)
P. Singer (ed.) *Companion to Ethics* (Blackwell 1993)
P. Singer (editor) *Applied Ethics* (Oxford University Press, 1986)
Society for the Protection of the Unborn Child *Love Your Unborn
    Neighbour* (SPUC, 1994)
The Church and the Bomb (CIO/Hodder, 1982)
P. Vardy and P. Grosch *The Puzzle of Ethics* (Fount, 1994).
Wilcockson, S. *Last Rights: Christian Perspectives on Euthanasia*
    (Grove, 1981).

Acknowledgements

I would like to thank especially the help of Selma Thomas and Lucy Stockwell (Eton College, School Library) in their provision of books and sources but particularly, Alison Wilcockson, wife, critic, proof reader and a constant source of encouragement.

Index